MAGIC RING

A Collection of Verse for Children

Edited by
RUTH A. BROWN

Revised by
H. JEAN BRECK

American Camping Association
Martinsville, Indiana

Careful research and investigation has been done to trace the poetry to the original source in order that proper copyright clearance could be made. In some cases, because of the obscurity of the original author, no claimant could be found. Despite the efforts made, if any copyright has been unknowingly infringed upon, we ask that the publisher be notified so that proper acknowledgements and permissions can be obtained.

ISBN # 0-87603-082-7
Copyright 1985 by American Camping Association
All Rights Reserved
Printed in the United States of America

Book Illustrations by
JO ANNE NORLING FERINGER

Cover by
TOM DOUGHERTY and STEVE CARRELL

To the Memory of
RUTH A. BROWN

CONTENTS

v

ACKNOWLEDGMENTS

*T*he campers and counselors who played Magic Ring and who wrote the poems and songs in the Sandalwood Box section are the main ones I have to thank for the existence of this third edition. Of course, there are others without whom I could not have done it and to whom I owe my thanks: Jo Anne Norling Feringer, who has captured the creative spirit and adventure of Four Winds and Westward Ho in her drawings; her father, Ernest Norling, an artist who enjoyed many evenings of Magic Ring and from whom the original ideas for three of the drawings were obtained; for help in selecting the poems and songs and for criticism and assistance I am indebted to Elizabeth Pritchard Jacobsen and her husband Joseph, to Peggy Schiff Enderlein, to my sister Marlys Swenson Waller, to Leslie Clark and her husband John, to Kathleen Skinner, and to my daughter Carole Breck. Finally, I am indebted to my understanding husband John and our son Allen for their support and encouragement.

The selections listed below are used by permission of, and special arrangements with, the following authorized publishers, editors and individual holders of copyright. Permission secured 1926 and for additional material 1937 by Ruth A. Brown.

The Atlantic Monthly, Boston, Massachusetts, for "A Blackbird Suddenly" and "Hill Hunger" by Joseph Auslander; "The Venture" by Jean Kenyon MacKenzie. Personal acknowledgment is also made to Mr. Auslander and Miss MacKenzie.

Bobbs-Merrill Company, for "A Parting Guest" and "A Sudden Shower" by James Whitcomb Riley.

Messrs. Brandt and Brandt, New York, for lines from "Renascence" and "Afternoon on a Hill" by Edna St. Vincent Millay from "Renascence and other Poems" published by Messrs. Harper and Bros., Publishers.

Messrs. Brentano, New York, for "Blind" and "Going Down in Ships" by Harry Kemp.

Jonathan Cape, Ltd., London, for "Leisure" and "Days Too Short" from Collected Poems by William H. Davies.

Mrs. Katharine M. Carruth, for "Each in His Own Tongue" by William Herbert Carruth.

The Century Company, New York, and Mr. Rice personally, for "The Immortal" and "Which" by Cale Young Rice.

Messrs. Chatto and Windus, Ltd., London, for "Ode" by Arthur William Edgar O'Shaughnessy.

The Chicago Daily News for "The Magic Window" by Eleanor Hammond.

The Churchman, New York, for "Countersign" by Arthur Ketchum.

Grace Hazard Conkling for "After Sunset."

Messrs. W. B. Conkey Company, Hammond, Indiana, for "The World's Need" by Ella Wheeler Wilcox.

Contemporary Verse, Norwalk, Connecticutt, for "God, You Have Been Too Good to Me" and "Standards" by Charles Wharton Stork.

J. M. Dent & Sons, Ltd., for "The Common Street" by Helen Gray Cone and "The Donkey" by Gilbert Keith Chesterton.

Messrs. Dodd, Mead and Company, New York, for "The Great Lover" by Rupert Brooke; "A Ballade-Catalogue of Lovely Things" and "I Meant to Do My Work Today" by Richard Le Gallienne.

Messrs. George H. Doran Company, New York, for "Herb of Grace," "Magic Night," "Rain in the Night," and "Romany Gold" by Amelia Josephine Burr; "Love's Lantern" by Aline Kilmer; "Easter" and "Roofs" by Joyce Kilmer; "Smells" by Christopher Morley; "Still Let Us Go the Way of Beauty" by Charles Hanson Towne; and "Clay Hills" by Jean Starr Untermeyer.

Messrs. E. P. Dutton and Company, New York, for "The Night Will Never Stay" by Eleanor Farjeon; "Friends" by W. Letts; and "The Builder" and "Creeds" by Willard Wattles.

Mr. Anthony Euwer for his poems, "The Forest" and "Imagination."

Rachel Field for her poems, "If Once You Have Slept on an Island" and "Islands."

Messrs. Harcourt, Brace and Company, Inc., New York, for "Primer Lesson" from Slabs of the Sunburnt West by Carl Sandburg; "Little Things" by Marian Strobel; "Prayer" and "Spring" by Louis Untermeyer.

Messrs. Harper and Brothers, New York, for "The Road to Vagabondia," "Song" and "Song for Youth" by Dana Burnet; "Canoe Trails," "Hills" and "Wind-in-the-Hair and Rain-in-the-Face" by Arthur Guiterman.

Harvard University Press for "Chorus from Hippolytus" by Euripides, translation by Gilbert Murray.

Messrs. Henry Holt and Company, New York, for "Whole Duty of Berkshire Brooks" by Grace Hazard Conkling; "Mending Wall," "The Mountains Are a Lonely Folk," "The Road Not Taken" and

"Stopping by Woods on a Snowy Evening" by Robert Frost; "Silver" by Walter de la Mare; and "Fog," "Masses" and "Monotone" by Carl Sandburg.

Messrs. Houghton, Mifflin Company, Boston, Massachusetts, for "Before the Rain," "Maple Leaves" and "Memory" by Thomas Bailey Aldrich; "Her Words" by Anna Hempstead Branch; "Fairy Ring" and "Windows" by Abbie Farwell Brown; "The Poetry of Earth" by Florence Earle Coates; "Holiness" and "A Town Window" by John Drinkwater; "I Have Come from the Spring Woods" and "The Snowstorm" by Ralph Waldo Emerson; "April" by Theodosia Garrison; "The Cedars," "The Golden Shoes" and "The House and the Road" by Josephine Preston Peabody; "My Wage," "The Secret" and "Windows" by Jessie B. Rittenhouse; "Daisies" and "Prayer" by Frank Dempster Sherman; "Window Song" by Nancy Shores; "The Peddler of Dreams" by Victor Starbuck; "Envoi" by William Roscoe Thayer; and "The Sandpiper" by Celia Thaxter.

Leslie Nelson Jennings for his poem, "Highways."

Messrs. Alfred A. Knopf, Inc., New York, for "Adventure," "Fate Defied and "On Seeing Weather Beaten Trees" by Adelaide Crapsey; "Truth" by Max Eastman; and "Little Things" by Orrick Johns.

Messrs. Little, Brown and Company, Boston, Massachusetts, for selections by Emily Dickinson.

Messrs. Lothrop, Lee and Shepard Company, Boston, Massachusetts, for "The Human Touch" by Richard Burton.

Messrs. MacMillan Company, New York, for "My Garden" by Thomas Edward Brown; "For a Child" and "Souls" by Fannie Stearns Davis; "The Leaden-Eyed," "A Net to Snare the Moonlight," and "The Sorceress" by Vachel Lindsay; "Cargoes," "Sea-Fever," and "The Wanderer's Song" by John Masefield; "Little Things" by James Stephens; "Barter," "The Coin," "The Cup," and "Leaves" by Sara Teasdale; "The Lake Isle of Innisfree," "Lyric from the Land of Heart's Desire" and "The Song of the Wandering Aengus" by William Butler Yeats.

Edwin Markham for his poems, "Brotherhood," "A Creed," "The Divine Strategy," "Man-Making," "Outwitted," and "Prayer."

Thomas B. Mosher for "Frost To-Night" by Edith M. Thomas.

The New York Sun for "Gifts" by Blanche Shoemaker Wagstaff.

The New York Times for "Hold Fast Your Dreams" by Louise Driscoll and to Miss Driscoll personally.

Messrs. G. P. Putnam's Sons, New York and London, for selections by David Morton.

Clinton Scollard for his poem, "Beauty."

Messrs. Charles Scribner's Sons, New York, for "Music I Heard" by Conrad Aiken; "Wind" by John Galsworthy; "A Ballad of Trees and the Master" by Sidney Lanier; "Cradle-Song at Twilight," "The Lady Poverty" and "The Shepherdess" by Alice Meynell, credit is also given to Wilfrid Meynell; "Stretch Out Your Hand" by Corinne Roosevelt Robinson; selections from the poems of Robert Louis Stevenson; "Birds" by Richard Henry Stoddard; "Four Things," "God of the Open Air," "Home Thoughts from Europe," and "Work" by Henry Van Dyke; and "Love of Life" by Tertius Van Dyke, Credit is also given to Mr. Tertius Van Dyke.

Frances Shaw for her poem, "Who Loves the Rain."

Messrs. Small, Maynard and Company, Boston, Massachusetts, for "An April Morning," lines from "The Joys of the Road," "Let Us Go in Once More," and "A Vagabond Song" by Bliss Carman; "The Sea Gypsy" and "The Wanderer" by Richard Hovey; and lines from "The Song of the Open Road" by Walt Whitman.

Miriam Vedder for her poem, "Conversations."

Rowe Wright for her poem, "A Prayer for November."

The Yale Review, Yale University Press for "A Clear Night," "Daily Bread," "Days" "Good Company," and "Morning Song" by Karle Wilson Baker; and lines from "Earth" by John Hall Wheelock.

THE TRADITION OF THE MAGIC RING

*M*agic Ring is a collection of poems loved by hundreds of girls and boys. Before it became a book, it was a poetry game, played by girls around camp fires and along mountain trails. The game started many years ago at Camp Sealth when the storyteller for evening fire was late. The first signs of autumn in the air reminded someone of a poem. She repeated it, and that recalled another and another poem about autumn. Those who knew the poems joined in. There was such a glow of happy interest on the ring of faces around the fire that the game went on until someone noticed it was time for the goodnight song.

"Wasn't that fun! It went like magic," exclaimed a young camper; and the game has been called Magic Ring ever since. Sealth, Four Winds and Westward Ho campers, counselors and friends have taken the game all over the United States.

As all things that are nurtured grow, so Magic Ring has grown apace. The game of Magic Ring grew to be one of the best loved games for evening fire and in girls' and boys' notebooks grew collections of their favorite verse and songs.

The more poems they loved, the more places they found where it was fun to say them. Sunny days on the deck of a sailboat invited them to poems of ships and the sea.

In many summer camps and schools the game, Magic Ring, is part of the daily program. It is particularly adapted to the summer camp. Sometimes a group in charge of morning assembly will ask the campers to meet at the "big rock" with poems about hills and mountains. At an evening fire, before a star gazing trip perhaps, they will bring poems about stars and night. Rain in the offing will bring everyone to the hearthside for a ceremony of wind and rain poems. Sometimes these poems are about common things, of adventuring, of nature, of love of being, or love of places.

The game is used in many schools either at a scheduled period or when the regular work is completed.

The favorite way to play the game is to have someone start a poem and all who know it join in saying it. Another way is for someone to say a poem and then call on another person to say one. A third way is for a person to volunteer and say a poem alone. A camper might stand up and say a poem previously selected by his or her tentmates. While on a hike, a cruise, or a canoe trip, the campers together with their counselors often write a log of their adventures. Sometimes these are set to music and sung to the rest of the camp upon their return. Some of the logs are beautifully illustrated. Some are dramatized.

In these ways the interest broadened, more girls and boys learned more poems, the notebook collections grew fatter and fatter until finally it was requested that a collection of Magic Ring poems be printed. Since the publication of that first edition most of the campers have started poetry shelves of their own—saving their money to buy new volumes.

The girls and boys who play Magic Ring will tell you that this love of poetry has given new color and interest to ordinary things. They have learned that poetry expresses for them thoughts and feelings they cannot express themselves. A poem is a way of expressing something central to man's existence, a feeling, an idea. It is a way of spiritual growth. It is a kind of universal language.

More than this it has put them on the alert for undiscovered beauty, which is reflected in their own original camp songs and verse. Included in this edition of *Magic Ring* are a group of poems and songs written by the campers and counselors.

Originally *Magic Ring* was edited by Ruth A. Brown. In 1976 Miss Brown requested that I revise and bring up-to-date this collection of verse to give pleasure to new generations of campers and counselors and make it available to a wider circle of children.

May boys and girls and grownups everywhere find here poems which will make everyday life more joyous and meaningful. To them we offer this volume with an invitation to play with us the game of Magic Ring.

—H. JEAN BRECK

WHO WALKS WITH BEAUTY

Who walks with Beauty has no need of fear;
   The sun and moon and stars keep pace with him.
Invisible hands restore the ruined year,
   And time, itself, grows beautifully dim.
One hill will keep the footprints of the moon,
   That came and went a hushed and secret hour;
One star at dusk will yield the lasting boon:
   Remembered Beauty's white, immortal flower.

Who takes of Beauty, wine and daily bread,
   Will know no lack when bitter years are lean;
The brimming cup is by, the feast is spread;
   The sun and moon and stars his eyes have seen,
Are for his hunger and the thirst he slakes:
   The wine of Beauty and the bread he breaks.

DAVID MORTON

LEISURE

What is this life if, full of care,
We have no time to stand and stare?

No time to stand beneath the boughs
And stare as long as sheep or cows.

No time to see, when woods we pass,
Where squirrels hide their nuts in grass.

No time to see, in broad daylight,
Streams full of stars, like skies at night.

No time to turn at Beauty's glance,
And watch her feet, how they can dance.

No time to wait till her mouth can
Enrich that smile her eyes began.

A poor life this if, full of care,
We have not time to stand and stare.

WILLIAM H. DAVIES

FOR A CHILD

Your friends shall be the Tall Wind,
  The River and the Tree;
The Sun that laughs and marches,
  The Swallows and the Sea.

Your prayers shall be the murmur
  Of grasses in the rain;
The song of wild wood thrushes
  That makes God glad again.

And you shall run and wander,
  And you shall dream and sing
Of brave things and bright things
  Beyond the swallow's wing.

And you shall envy no man,
  Nor hurt your heart with sighs,
For I will keep you simple
  That God may make you wise.

FANNY STEARNS DAVIS

"LOVELIEST OF TREES, THE CHERRY NOW"

Loveliest of trees, the cherry now
Is hung with bloom along the bough,
And stands about the woodland ride
Wearing white for Eastertide.

Now, of my threescore years and ten,
Twenty will not come again,
And take from seventy springs a score,
It only leaves me fifty more.

And since to look at things in bloom
Fifty springs are little room,
About the woodlands I will go
To see the cherry hung with snow.

A. E. HOUSMAN

HOLINESS

If all the carts were painted gay,
   And all the streets swept clean,
And all the children came to play
   By hollyhocks, with green
   Grasses to grow between,

If all the houses looked as though
   Some heart were in their stones,
If all the people that we know
   Were dressed in scarlet gowns,
   With feathers in their crowns,

I think this gaiety would make
   A spiritual land.
I think that holiness would take
   This laughter by the hand,
   Till both should understand.

JOHN DRINKWATER

A FINE DAY

Clear had the day been from the dawn,
All chequer'd was the sky,
Thin clouds like scarfs of cobweb lawn
Veil'd heaven's most glorious eye.
The wind had no more strength than this,
That leisurely it blew,
To make one leaf the next to kiss
That closely by it grew.

MICHAEL DRAYTON

I lost a world the other day.
Has anybody found?
You'll know it by the row of stars
Around its forehead bound.

A rich man might not notice it;
Yet to my frugal eye
Of more esteem than ducats.
Oh, find it, sir, for me!

EMILY DICKINSON

BEAUTY

You bid me stay; I go
Whither no man may know.

I am the rose's soul,
The breast of the oriole.

I am the rainbow's arc,
The star on the breast of the dark.

Sever me, I am still
The wonder on the hill.

Part me, and I am yet
The heart of the violet.

With the first flush of morn
I am each day re-born.

CLINTON SCOLLARD

BARTER

Life has loveliness to sell,
All beautiful and splendid things,
Blue waves whitened on a cliff,
Soaring fire that sways and sings,
And children's faces looking up
Holding wonder like a cup.

Life has loveliness to sell,
Music like a curve of gold,
Scent of pine trees in the rain,
Eyes that love you, arms that hold,
And for your spirit's still delight,
Holy thoughts that star the night.

Spend all you have for loveliness,
Buy it and never count the cost;
For one white singing hour of peace
Count many a year of strife well lost,
And for a breath of ecstasy
Give all you have been, or could be.

SARA TEASDALE

A BALLADE-CATALOGUE OF LOVELY THINGS

I would make a list against the evil days
Of lovely things to hold in memory:
First I set down my lady's lovely face,
    For earth has no such lovely thing as she;
    And next I add, to bear her company,
The great-eyed virgin star that morning brings;
    Then the wild-rose upon its little tree—
So runs my catalogue of lovely things.

The enchanted dogwood, with its ivory trays,
    The water-lily in its sanctuary
Of reeded pools, and dew-drenched lilac sprays,
    For these, of all fair flowers, the fairest be;
    Next write I down the great name of the sea,
Lonely in greatness as the names of kings;
    Then the young moon that has us all in fee—
So runs my catalogue of lovely things.

Imperial sunsets that in crimson blaze
    Along the hills, and, fairer still to me,
The fireflies dancing in a netted maze
    Woven of twilight and tranquility;
    Shakespeare and Virgil, their high poesy;
Then a great ship, splendid with snowy wings,
    Voyaging on into eternity—
So runs my catalogue of lovely things.

Envoi

Prince, not the gold bars of thy treasury,
    Not all thy jewelled sceptres, crowns and rings,
Are worth the honeycomb of the wild bee—
    So runs my catalogue of lovely things.

RICHARD LE GALLIENNE

What is lovely never dies, but passes into
    other loveliness,
Stardust, or sea foam, flower or winged air.
A shadow of the night.

THOMAS BAILEY ALDRICH

FROM ENDYMION

A thing of beauty is a joy forever:
Its loveliness increases; it will never
Pass into nothingness, but still will keep
A bower quiet for us, and sleep
Full of sweet dreams, and health and quiet breathing.
Therefore, on every morrow, are we wreathing
A flowery band to bind us to the earth.

JOHN KEATS

TOP O' THE WORLD

Top o' the hill my house is built,
  And top o' the house live I—
Up with the sound of the tree-tuned lilt
Of the wind to the deep night sky.

And whether it cloud or whether it shine,
  Alone with my wind and my sky,
I can dream the dreams that are mine, all mine,
  Top o' the world till I die!

LESLIE VARICK PERKINS

SIC VITA

Heart free, hand free,
Blue above, brown under,
All the world to me
Is a place of wonder.
Sunshine, moonshine,
Stars, and winds a-blowing,
All into this heart of mine
Flowing, flowing, flowing.

Mind free, step free,
Days to follow after,
Joys of life sold to me
For the price of laughter.
Girl's love, man's love,
Love of work and duty;
Just a way of God's to prove
Beauty, beauty, beauty.

WILLIAM STANLEY BRAITHWAITE

FROM THE GREAT LOVER

These I have loved:

          White plates and cups, clean-gleaming,
Ringed with blue lines; and feathery, faery dust;
Wet roofs, beneath the lamp-light; the strong crust
Of friendly bread; and many-tasting food;
Rainbows; and the blue bitter smoke of wood;
And radiant raindrops couching in cool flowers;
And flowers themselves, that sway through sunny hours,
Dreaming of moths that drink them under the moon;
Then, the cool kindliness of sheets, that soon
Smooth away trouble; and the rough male kiss
Of blankets; grainy wood; live hair that is
Shining and free; blue-massing clouds; the keen
Unpassioned beauty of a great machine;
The benison of hot water; furs to touch;
The good smell of old clothes; and other such—
The comfortable smell of friendly fingers,
Hair's fragrance, and the musty reek that lingers
About dead leaves and last year's ferns . . .
                      Dear names,
And thousand others throng to me! Royal flames:
Sweet water's dimpling laugh from tap or spring;
Holes in the ground; and voices that do sing;
Voices in laughter, too; and body's pain,
Soon turned to peace; and the deep-panting train;
Firm sands; the little dulling edge of foam
That browns and dwindles as the wave goes home;
And washen stones, gay for an hour; the cold
Graveness of iron; moist black earthen mold;
Sleep; and high places; footprints in the dew;
And oaks; and brown horse-chestnuts, glossy new;
And new-peeled sticks; and shining pools on grass.
All these have been my loves and these shall pass,
Whatever passes not, in the great hour,
Nor all my passion, all my prayers, have power
To hold them with me through the gate of Death.
They'll play deserter, turn the traitor breath,
Break the high bond we made, and sell Love's trust
And sacramented covenant to dust.
—Oh, never doubt but, somewhere, I shall wake,
And give what's left of love again, and make

New friends, now strangers . . .
But the best I've known,
Stays here, and changes, breaks, grows old, is blown
About the winds of the world, and fades from brains
Of living men, and dies.
Nothing remains.
O dear my loves, O faithless, once again
This one last gift I give; that after men
Shall know, and later lovers, far-removed,
Praise you, "All these were lovely;" say, "He loved."

RUPERT BROOKE

THE PEDDLER OF DREAMS

Here are wondrous things to buy,
April mist and summer sky,
Rhymes and dreams of quaint device,
Slanting sails and fairy rings,
Comet tails and swallow wings,
Roads that run to paradise.

Who will buy a little dream, a dream of open spaces
Where the clouds go drifting white above the stream?
Who will buy an April wind out of woodland places?
There is magic in my pack—
Who will buy a dream?

Here we have a shining sail dropping like a swallow
Dim against the skyline when the twilights fail,
Beating out to tropic Isles where the sea-gulls follow
Golden in the sea dawns;
Who will buy a sail?

Something novel in a road, a road whereon to wander;
A road that leads to Camelot, to Nineveh and Tyre.
Through meadows where the daffodils have minted gold to
squander.
Who will buy the quiet road that leads to Heart's desire?

Who will buy the Kingdom and the glory and the power?
Look at this, a crescent moon above a country lane.
See the drooping beauty of this cherry tree in flower—

In my pack are wondrous things—
Mermaid-scales and dodo-wings.
Folk are buying shoes and ships—
Books and breads and ladies' lips;
All day long my wares I cry,
No one heeds me, none will buy.

VICTOR STARBUCK

SEA

Only to hear and see the far-off sparkling brine,
Only to hear were sweet, stretched out beneath the pine.
From, "The Song of the Lotos-Eaters"
ALFRED TENNYSON

GIFTS

For these let me be thankful on this day:
Warm spreading sun and flowers that brightly bloom,
The breath of scented springtime in my room.
The open sky of blue above my way—
Swift winds that sweep the clouds across the bay
And sounds that pulse the earth with sudden song:
Peepers, and whippoorwills and birds whose long
Sweet notes spill golden harmonies of May;
These but the symbols of a greater thing—
The warm blood in my veins, the eager heart
That at each touch of Beauty feels the start
Of fine resurgence-quickened as the spring,
Yea, above all, oh let me greatly prize
The Gift of Life, supreme, through Beauty's eyes!
BLANCHE SHOEMAKER WAGSTAFF

WINDOWS

The windows of the place wherein I dwell
I will make beautiful. No garish light
Shall enter crudely; but with colors bright
And warm and throbbing I will weave a spell,
In rainbow harmony the theme to tell
Of sage and simple saint and noble knight,
Beggar and king who fought the gallant fight;
These will transfigure even my poor cell.

But when the shadows of the night begin,
And sifted sunlight falls no more on me,
May I have learned to light my lamp within;
So that the passing world may look and see
Still the same radiance, though with paler hue
Of the sweet lives that help men to live true.

ABBIE FARWELL BROWN

Still let us go the way of beauty; go
The way of loveliness; still let us know
Those paths that lead where Pan and Daphne run,
Where roses prosper in the summer sun.

CHARLES HANSON TOWNE

SONG FOR YOUTH

Gather all the sweet of May,
Lock it tenderly away,
Precious night and perfect day.

Make a trove of shining things,
Roses, raindrops, dreams, and wings;
Catch a skylark while he sings!

Gather all the summer's sweet,
Hush of heaven, song of street,
Stars that dance on silver feet!

Then grow old with gallant ease,
For I am told such wealths as these
Make the fairest memories!

DANA BURNET

GOD OF THE OPEN AIR

These are the gifts I ask
Of thee, Spirit serene:
Strength for the daily task,
Courage to face the road,
Good cheer to help me bear the traveller's load,
And, for the hours of rest that come between,
An inward joy in all things heard and seen.

These are the things I prize
And hold of dearest worth:
Light of the sapphire skies,
Peace of the silent hills,
Shelter of forests, comfort of the grass,
Music of birds, murmur of little rills,
Shadows of cloud that swiftly pass
And, after showers,
The smell of flowers
And of the good brown earth—
And best of all, along the way, friendship and mirth.

HENRY VAN DYKE

ASOLO

Day!
Faster and more fast,
O'er night's brim, day boils at last:
Boils, pure gold, o'er the cloud-cup's brim
Where spurting and suppressed it lay,
For not a froth-flake touched the rim
Of yonder gap in the solid gray
Of the eastern cloud, an hour away;
But forth one wavelet, then another, curled,
Till the whole sunrise, not to be suppressed,
Rose, reddened, and its seething breast
Flickered in bounds, grew gold, then overflowed the world.
Oh Day, if I squander a wavelet of thee,
A mite of my twelve-hours' treasure,
The least of thy gaze or glances,
(Be they grants thou art bound to or gifts above measure)
One of thy choices or one of thy chances,
(Be they tasks God imposed thee or freaks at thy pleasure)
—My Day, if I squander such labor or leisure,
Then shame fall on Asolo, mischief on me!

ROBERT BROWNING

MEMORY

My mind lets go a thousand things,
Like dates of wars and deaths of kings,
And yet recalls the very hour—
'Twas noon by yonder village tower,
And on the last blue noon in May—
The wind came briskly up this way,
Crisping the brook beside the road;
Then, pausing here, set down its load
Of pine-scents, and shook listlessly
Two petals from that wild-rose tree.

THOMAS BAILEY ALDRICH

"Tho' we travel the world over to find the beautiful,
We must carry it with us or we find it not."

RALPH WALDO EMERSON

LOVE OF LIFE

Love you not the tall trees spreading wide their branches,
     Cooling with their green shade the sunny days of June?
Love you not the little bird lost among the leaflets,
     Dreamily repeating a quaint, brief tune?

Is there not a joy in the waste windy places?
     Is there not a song by the long dusty way?
Is there not a glory in the sudden hour of struggle?
     Is there not a peace in the long quiet day?

Love you not the meadows with their deep lush grasses?
     Love you not the cloud-flock noiseless in their flight?
Love you not the cool wind that stirs to meet the sunrise?
     Love you not the stillness of the warm summer night?

Have you never wept with a grief that slowly passes?
     Have you never laughed when a joy goes running by?
Know you not the peace of rest that follows labor?
     You have not learned to live then; how can you dare
          to die?

TERTIUS VAN DYKE

THE MAGIC WINDOW

Our window is a magic frame
With pictures never twice the same.
Sometimes it frames a sunset sky,
Where clouds of gold and purple lie.
And sometimes, on a windless night,
It holds a great moon round and white.
Sometimes it frames a lawn and flowers,
Where children play through summer hours.
Sometimes, a tree of gold and red
And grass where cripst brown leaves are shed.
And sometimes it shows wind-blown rain
Or snowflakes against the pane.
Our window frames all lovely things
That every changing season brings.

ELEANOR HAMMOND

AFTERNOON ON A HILL

I will be the gladdest thing
    Under the sun!
I will touch a hundred flowers
    And not pick one.

I will look at cliffs and clouds .
    With quiet eyes,
Watch the wind bow down the grass,
    And the grass rise.

And when the lights begin to show
    Up from the town,
I will mark which must be mine,
    And then start down!

EDNA ST. VINCENT MILLAY

"GOD, YOU HAVE BEEN TOO GOOD TO ME"

God, you have been too good to me,
    You don't know what You've done.
A cloud's too small to drink in all
    The treasure of the sun.

The pitcher fills the lifted cup
    And still the blessings pour;
They overbrim the shallow rim
    With cool refreshing store.

You are too prodigal with joy,
    Too careless of its worth,
To let the stream with crystal gleam
    Fall wasted on the earth.

Let many thirsty lips draw near
    And quaff the greater part!
There still will be too much for me
    To hold in one glad heart.

                  CHARLES WHARTON STORK

THE WORLD

Great, wide, beautiful, wonderful World,
With the wonderful water round you curled,
And the wonderful grass upon your breast—
World, you are beautifully drest!

The wonderful air is over me,
And the wonderful wind is shaking the trees;
It walks on the water, and whirls the mills,
And talks to itself on the tops of the hills.

Your friendly Earth, how far do you go,
With the wheat-fields that nod and the rivers that flow,
With cities and gardens, and cliffs and isles,
And people upon you for thousands of miles?

Ah, you are so great, and I am so small,
I tremble to think of you, World, at all;
And yet, when I said my prayers today,
A whisper inside me seemed to say,
"You are more than the earth, though you are such a dot:
You can love and think, and the Earth cannot."

                  W. B. RANDS

EVERYTHING THAT I CAN SPY

Everything that I can spy
Through the circle of my eye,
Everything that I can see
Has been woven out of me.
I have sown the stars; I threw
Clouds of morn and noon and eve
In the deeps and steeps of blue;
And each thing that I perceive,
Sun and sea and mountain high,
Are made and moulded by my eye;
Closing it, I do but find
Darkness, and a little wind.

JAMES STEPHENS

SMELLS

Why is it that the poets tell
So little of the sense of smell?
These are the odors I love well:

The smell of coffee freshly ground;
Or rich plum pudding, holly crowned;
Or onions fried and deeply browned.

The fragrance of a fumy pipe;
The smell of apples newly ripe;
Of printers' ink on leaden type.

Woods by moonlight in September
Breathe most sweet; and I remember
Many a smoky campfire ember.

Camphor, turpentine, and tea,
The balsam of a Christmas tree,
These are whiffs of gramarye . . .
A ship smells best of all to me!

CHRISTOPHER MORLEY

TREASURES

Down on the beach when the tide is out
Beautiful things lie all about—
Rubies and diamonds and shells and pearls,
Starfish, oysters and mermaids' curls;
Slabs of black marble cut in sand,
Veined and smoothed and polished by hand;
And whipped-up foam that I think must be
What mermen use for cream in tea.
These and a million treasures I know
Strew the beach when the tide is low—
But very few people seem to care
For such gems scattered everywhere.
Lots of these jewels I hide away
In an old box I found one day.
And if a begger asks me for bread
I will give him diamonds instead.

MARY DIXON THAYER

HAD I A GOLDEN POUND

Had I a golden pound to spend,
My love should mend and sew no more.
And I would buy her a little quern,
Easy to turn on the kitchen floor.

And for her windows curtains white,
With birds in flight and flowers in bloom,
To face with pride the road to town,
And mellow down her sunlit room.

And with silver change we'd prove
The truth of Love to Life's own end,
With hearts the years could but embolden,
Had I a golden pound to spend.

FRANCIS LEDWIDGE

I MEANT TO DO MY WORK TODAY

I meant to do my work today—
  But a brown bird sang in the apple tree
And a butterfly flitted across the field,
  And all the leaves were calling me.

And the wind went sighing over the land,
  Tossing the grasses to and fro,
And a rainbow held out its shining hand—
So what could I do but laugh and go?

RICHARD LE GALLIENNE

LITTLE THINGS

Little things I'll give to you
Till your fingers learn to press
Gently
On a loveliness.

Little things and new—
Till your fingers learn to hold
Love that's fragile,
Love that's old.

MARIAN STROBEL

LET ME GO WHERE'ER I WILL

Let me go where'er I will,
I hear a sky-born music still:
It sounds from all things old,
It sounds from all things young,
From all that's fair, from all that's foul,
Peals out a cheerful song.
It is not only in the rose,
It is not only in the bird,
Not only where the rainbow glows,
Nor in the song of woman heard,
But in the darkest, meanest things
There alway, alway something sings.
'Tis not in the high stars alone,
Nor in the cups of budding flowers,
Nor in the red-breast's mellow tone,
Nor in the bow that smiles in showers,
But in the mud and scum of things
There alway, alway something sings.

RALPH WALDO EMERSON

THE COMMON STREET

The common street climbed up against the sky,
  Gray meeting gray; and wearily to and fro
  I saw the patient common people go,
Each, with his sordid burden, trudging by.

And the rain dropped; there was not any sigh
  Or stir of a live wind; dull, dull and slow
  All motion; as a tale told long ago
The faded world; and creeping night drew nigh.

Then burst the sunset, flooding far and fleet,
  Leavening the whole of life with magic leaven.
  Suddenly down the long, wet, glistening hill
Pure splendor poured—and lo! the common street,
  A golden highway into golden heaven
  With the dark shapes of men ascending still.

HELEN GRAY CONE

HOLD FAST YOUR DREAMS

Hold fast your dreams!
Within your heart
Keep one, still, secret spot
Where dreams may go,
And sheltered so,
May thrive and grow—
Where doubt and fear are not.
O, keep a place apart,
Within your heart,
For little dreams to go!

LOUISE DRISCOLL

And I too sing the song of all creation,
  A brave sky, and a glad wind blowing by,
A clear trail and an hour for meditation,
  A long day, and the joy to make it fly ;
A hard task and the muscles to achieve it,
  A fierce noon and a well-contented gloam,
A good strife and no great regret to leave it,
  A still night and the far red lights of home.

HERBERT BASHFORD

FATE DEFIED

As it
Were tissue of silver
I'll wear, O fate, thy grey,
And go mistily radiant, clad
Like the moon.

ADELAIDE CRAPSEY

TO ARCADY

Across the hills of Arcady
    Into the Land of Song—
Ah, dear, if you will go with me
    The way will not be long.

It does not lie through solitudes
    Of wind-blown woods or sea;
Dear, no! the city's weariest moods
    May scarce veil Arcady.

'Tis no unfamiliar land
    Lit by some distant star;
See! Arcady is where you stand,
    And song is where you are.

Then go but hand in hand with me—
    No road can lead us wrong;
Here are the hills of Arcady—
    This is the Land of Song.

CHARLES BUXTON GOING

LITTLE THINGS

There's nothing very beautiful and nothing very gay
About the rush of faces in the town by day,
But a light tan cow in a pale green mead,
That is very beautiful, beautiful indeed . . .
And the soft March wind, and the low March mist
Are better than kisses in the dark street kissed . . .
The fragrance of the forest when it wakes at dawn,
The fragrance of a trim green village lawn,
The hearing of the murmur of the rain at play—
These things are beautiful, beautiful as day!
And I shan't stand waiting for love or scorn
When the feast is laid for a day new-born . . .
Oh, better let the little things I loved when little
Return when the heart finds the great things brittle;
And better is a temple made of bark and thong
Than a tall stone temple that may stand too long.

ORRICK JOHNS

THE SHEPHERDESS

She walks—the lady of my delight—
    A shepherdess of sheep.
Her flocks are thoughts. She keeps them white;
    She guards them from the steep.
She feeds them on the fragrant height,
    And folds them in for sleep.

She roams maternal hills and bright,
    Dark valleys safe and deep.
Her dreams are innocent at night;
    The chastest stars may peep.
She walks—the lady of my delight—
    A shepherdess of sheep.

She holds her little thoughts in sight,
    Though gay they run and leap.
She is so circumspect and right;
    She has her soul to keep.
She walks—the lady of my delight—
    A shepherdess of sheep.

ALICE MEYNELL

HERB OF GRACE

I do not know what sings in me—
  I only know it sings
When pale the stars, and every tree
  Is glad with waking wings.

I only know the air is sweet
  With wondrous flowers unseen—
That unaccountably complete
  Is June's accustomed green.

The wind has magic in its touch;
  Strange dreams the sunsets give.
Life I have questioned overmuch—
  Today, I live.

AMELIA JOSEPHINE BURR

HER WORDS

My mother has the prettiest tricks
  Of words and words and words.
Her talk comes out as smooth and sleek
  As breasts of singing birds.

She shapes her speech all silver fine
  Because she loves it so.
And her own eyes begin to shine
  To hear her stories grow.

And if she goes to make a call
  Or out to take a walk,
We leave our work when she returns
  And run to hear her talk.

We had not dreamed these things were so
  Of sorrow and of mirth.
Her speech is as a thousand eyes
  Through which we see the earth.

God wove a web of loveliness,
  Of clouds and stars and birds,
But made not anything at all
  So beautiful as words.

They shine around our simple earth
  With golden shadowings,
And every common thing they touch
  Is exquisite with wings.

There's nothing poor and nothing small
  But is made fair with them.
They are the hands of living faith
  That touch the garment's hem.

They are as fair as bloom or air,
  They shine like any star,
And I am rich who learned from her
  How beautiful they are.

ANNA HEMPSTEAD BRANCH

STRETCH OUT YOUR HAND

.Stretch out your hand and take the world's wide gift
Of Joy and Beauty. Open wide your soul
To God's supreme Creation; make it yours,
And give to other hearts your ample store;
For when the whole of you is but a part
Of joyous beauty such as e'er endures,
Only by giving can you gain the more!

CORINNE ROOSEVELT ROBINSON

TO K. De M.

A lover of the moorland bare,
And honest country winds you were;
The silver-skimming rain you took;
And loved the floodings of the brook,
Dew, frost and mountains, fire and seas,
Tumultuary silences,
Winds that in darkness fifed a tune,
And the high-riding, virgin moon.

And as the berry, pale and sharp,
Springs on some ditch's counterscarp
In our ungenial, native north—
You put your frosted wildings forth,
And on the heath, afar from man,
A strong and bitter virgin ran.

The berry ripened keeps the rude
And racy flavour of the wood.
And you that loved the empty plain
All redolent of wind and rain,
Around you still the curlew sings—
The freshness of the weather clings—
The maiden jewels of the rain
Sit in your dabbled locks again.

ROBERT LOUIS STEVENSON

THE LADY POVERTY

The Lady Poverty was fair:
But she has lost her looks of late,
With change of times and change of air,
Ah slattern! she neglects her hair,
Her gown, her shoes; she keeps no state
As once when her pure feet were bare.

Or—almost worse, if worse can be—
She scolds in parlours, dusts and trims,
Watches and counts. Oh, is this she
Whom Francis met, whose step was free,
Who with Obedience carolled hymns,
In Umbria walked with Chastity?

Where is her ladyhood? Not here,
Not among modern kinds of men;
But in the stony fields, where clear
Through the thin trees the skies appear,
In delicate spare soil and fen,
And slender landscape and austere.

ALICE MEYNELL

A LITTLE SONG OF LIFE

Glad that I live am I;
   That the sky is blue;
Glad for the country lanes,
   And the fall of dew.

After the sun the rain,
   After the rain the sun;
This is the way of life,
   Till the work be done.

All that we need to do,
   Be we low or high,
Is to see that we grow
   Nearer the sky.

LIZETTE WOODWORTH REESE

AUTUMN TEA TIME

The late light falls across the floor,
Turned amber from a yellow tree,—
And there are yellow cups for four,
And lemon for the tea.

The maples, like a million flames,
Have lit the golden afternoon,
An ambient radiance that shames
The ineffective noon . . .

Till dull and smoky greys return,
Quenching the street with chills and damps—
Leaving these asters where they burn,
Mellow like evening lamps.

DAVID MORTON

THE DAY WILL BRING SOME LOVELY THING

The day will bring some lovely thing,
I say it over each new dawn—
Some gay, adventurous thing to hold
Within my heart when it is gone,
And so I rise and go to meet
The day, with wings upon my feet.

I come upon it unaware,
Some hidden beauty without name,
A snatch of song, a breath of pine,
A poem lit with golden flame,
High-tangled bird notes, keenly thinned,
Like flying color on the wind.

No day has ever failed me quite;
Before the grayest day is done,
I come upon some misty bloom,
Or a late line of crimson sun.
Each night I pause, remembering
Some gay, adventurous, lovely thing.

GRACE NOLL CROWELL

HANDS

Tempest without: within the mellow glow
Of mingling lamp and firelight over all—
Etchings and water-colors on the wall,
Cushions and curtains of clear indigo,
Rugs, damask red and blue as Tyrian seas,
Deep chairs, black oaken settles, hammered brass,
Translucent porcelain and sea-green glass—
Color and warmth and light and dreamy ease:
And I sit wondering where are now the hands
That wrought at anvil, easel, wheel and loom—
Hands, slender, suave, red, gnarled—in foreign lands
Or English shops to furnish this seemly room;
And all the while, without, the windy rain
Drums like dead fingers tapping at the pane.

WILFRED WILSON GIBSON

THE BLOOM ON THE YOUNG BAMBOO

Who has seen in the Jungle
The bloom on the young bamboo?
Who has touched it softly
The green with the bloom of blue?

The butterflies' wings have touched it
As they came flittering through.
Thousands of wings have painted
The bloom of the young bamboo.

MARGARET REED

THE CUP

I cannot die who drink delight
From the cup of the crescent moon
And hungrily as men eat bread
Love the scented nights of June.

The rest may die but is there not
Some shining strange escape for me
Who find in beauty the bright wine
Of immortality?

SARA TEASDALE

GRATITUDE

These are the things I'm grateful for
  upon Thanksgiving Day—
The gentle voices of my friends,
 The kindly words they say.
The pleasant books that I have read,
The places I have known,
The memories that come to me
When I'm alone.

These are the things I'm grateful for
  upon Thanksgiving Day—
The color of the sunset sky,
Before it turns to gray.
The first shy flowers of spring,
The flaming leaves of fall—
The music of a meadow brook,
A night bird's call.

These are the things I'm grateful for
  upon Thanksgiving Day—
Pale snow that settles on the earth,
The cloudless blue of May.
The faiths that I have never lost,
The dreams for which I strive—
The knowledge, like a thread of song,
That I'm alive!

              ELIZABETH CHISHOLM

THE POETRY OF EARTH

There is always room for beauty; memory
  A myriad lovely blossoms may enclose,
But, whatsoe'er hath been, there still must be
  Room for another rose.

Though skylark, throstle, whitethroat, whip-poor-will,
  And nightingale earth's echoing chantries throng,
When comes another singer, there will be
  Room for another song.

              FLORENCE EARLE COATES

FROM "RENASCENCE"

The world stands out on either side
No wider than the heart is wide;
Above the world is stretched the sky,—
No higher than the soul is high.
The heart can push the sea and land
Farther away on either hand;
The soul can split the sky in two,
And let the face of God shine through.
But East and West will pinch the heart
Than can not keep them pushed apart;
And he whose soul is flat—the sky
Will cave in on him by and by.

EDNA ST. VINCENT MILLAY

DAYS

Some days my thoughts are just cocoons—all cold, and dull, and
  blind;
They hang from dripping branches in the grey woods of my mind;
And other days they drift and shine—such free and flying things,
I find the gold-dust in my hair, left by their brushing wings.

KARLE WILSON BAKER

MASSES

Among the mountains I wandered and saw blue haze and red crag
  and was amazed;
On the beach, where the long push under the endless tide maneuvers,
  I stood silent;
Under the stars on the prairie watching the Dipper slant over the
  horizon's edge, I was full of thoughts.
Great men, pageants of war and labor, soldiers and workers, mothers
  lifting their children — these all I touched, and felt the
  solemn thrill of them.

And then one day I got a true look at the Poor, millions of the
  Poor, patient and toiling; more patient than crags, tides, and
  stars; innumerable, patient as the darkness of night — and all
  broken, humble ruins of nations.

CARL SANDBURG

ESCAPE AT BEDTIME

The lights from the parlor and kitchen shone out
　Through the blinds and windows and bars;
And high overhead and all moving about,
　There are thousands of millions of stars.
There ne'er were such thousands of leaves on a tree,
　Nor of people in church or the Park,
As the crowds of the stars that looked down upon me,
　And that glittered and winked in the dark.
The Dog, and the Plough, and the Hunter, and all,
　And the star of the sailor, and Mars.
These shone in the sky, and the pail by the wall
　Would be half full of water and stars.
They saw me at last, and they chased me with cries,
　And they soon had me packed into bed;
But the glory kept shining and bright in my eyes,
　And the stars going round in my head.

ROBERT LOUIS STEVENSON

FIREFLIES

Little lamps of the dusk,
　You fly low and gold
When the summer evening
　Starts to unfold,
So that all the insects,
　Now, before you pass,
Will have light to see by
　Undressing in the grass.

But when night has flowered,
　Little lamps a-gleam,
You fly over tree-tops
　Following a dream.
Men wonder from their windows
　That a firefly goes so far—
They do not know your longing
　To be a shooting star.

CAROLYN HALL

ODE TO SOLITUDE

Happy the man, whose wish and care
A few paternal acres bound,
Content to breathe his native air
In his own ground.

Whose herds with milk, whose fields with bread,
Whose flocks supply him with attire,
Whose trees in summer yield him shade,
In winter fire.

Blest who can unconcern'dly find
Hours, days and years slide soft away.
In health of body, peace of mind,
Quiet by day,

Sound sleep by night; study and ease,
Together mix'd; sweet recreation,
And innocence, which most does please,
With meditation.

Thus let me live, unseen, unknown;
Thus unlamented let me die,
Steal from the world, and not a stone
Tell where I lie.

ALEXANDER POPE

A PARTING GUEST

What delightful hosts are they—
Life and Love!
Lingeringly I turn away,
This late hour, yet glad enough
They have not withheld from me
Their high hospitality.
So, with face lit with delight
And all gratitude, I stay
Yet to press their hands and say,
"Thanks.—So fine a time! Good night."

JAMES WHITCOMB RILEY

THE EARTH AND THE MAN

A little sun, a little rain,
   A soft wind blowing from the west—
And woods and fields are sweet again,
   And warmth within the mountain's breast.

So simple is the earth we tread,
   So quick with love and life her frame:
Ten thousand years have dawned and fled,
   And still her magic is the same.

A little love, a little trust,
   A soft impulse, a sudden dream—
And life as dry as desert dust
   Is fresher than a mountain stream.

So simple is the heart of man,
   So ready for new hope and joy:
Ten thousand years since it began
   Have left it younger than a boy.

STOPFORD AUGUSTUS BROOKE

TO A LITTLE GIRL

You taught me ways of gracefulness and fashions of address,
The mode of plucking pansies and the art of sowing cress,
And how to handle puppies, with propitiatory pats
For mother dogs, and little acts of courtesy to cats.

O connoisseur of pebbles, colored leaves and trickling rills,
Whom seasons fit as do the sheaths that wrap the daffodils,
Whose eyes' divine expectancy foretells some starry goal,
You taught me here docility—and how to save my soul.

HELEN PARRY EDEN

IMAGINATION

Give me imagination, Lord,
   To see the unseen things—
To know the yonder, far-off feel
   That comes when some bird sings.

ANTHONY EUWER

LAUGHING SONG

When the green woods laugh with the voice of joy,
And the dimpling stream runs laughing by,
When the air does laugh with our merry wit,
And the green hill laughs with the noise of it;

When the meadows laugh with lively green,
And the grasshopper laughs in the merry scene,
When Mary and Susan and Emily
With their sweet round mouths sing Ha, ha, he!

When the painted birds laugh in the shade,
When our table with cherries and nuts is spread,
Come live and be happy and join with me
To sing the sweet chorus of Ha, ha, he!

WILLIAM BLAKE

BIRDS

Birds are singing round my window
    Songs the sweetest ever heard,
And I hang my cage there daily,
    But I never catch a bird.

So with thoughts my brain is peopled,
    And they sing there all day long,
But they will not fold their pinions
    In the little cage of song.

RICHARD HENRY STODDARD

A CHILD'S GRACE

Here a little child I stand
Heaving up my either hand.
Cold as Paddocks though they be,
Here I lift them up to Thee,
For a Benizon to fall
On our meat, and on us all.

ROBERT HERRICK

PRAYER

Teach me, Father, how to go
Softly as the grasses grow;
Hush my soul to meet the shock
Of the wide world as a rock;
But my spirit, propt with power,
Make as simple as a flower,
Let the dry heart fill its cup,
Like a poppy looking up;
Let life lightly wear her crown,
Like a poppy looking down.

Teach me, Father, how to be
Kind and patient as a tree.
Joyfully the crickets croon
Under shady oak at noon;
Beetle, on his mission bent,
Tarries in that cooling tent.
Let me, also, cheer a spot,
Hidden field or garden grot—
Place where passing souls can rest
On the way and be their best.

EDWIN MARKHAM

FAITH

Better trust all and be deceived
 And weep that trust and that deceiving
Than doubt one heart that if believed
 Had blessed one's life with true believing.
Oh, in this mocking world, too fast
 The doubting friend o'ertakes our youth,
Better be cheated to the last
 Than lose the blessed hope of truth.

FRANCES ANNE KEMBLE

ON SEEING WEATHER-BEATEN TREES

Is it as plainly in our living shown,
By slant and twist, which way the wind has blown?

ADELAIDE CRAPSEY

THE WORLD IS TOO MUCH WITH US

The world is too much with us; late and soon,
Getting and spending, we lay waste our powers:
Little we see in Nature that is ours;
We have given our hearts away, a sordid boon!
This sea that bares her bosom to the moon,
The winds that will be howling at all hours,
And are up-gathered now like sleeping flowers;
For this, for everything, we are out of tune;
It moves us not.—Great God! I'd rather be
A Pagan suckled in a creed outworn;
So might I, standing on this pleasant lea,
Have glimpses that would make me less forlorn;
Have sight of Proteus rising from the sea;
Or hear old Triton blow his wreathed horn.

WILLIAM WORDSWORTH

A BOOK

There is no frigate like a book
    To take us lands away,
Nor any courser like a page
    Of prancing poetry.
This traverse may the poorest take
    Without oppress of toll;
How frugal is the chariot
    That bears a human soul!

EMILY DICKINSON

I'M GLAD

I'm glad the sky is painted blue,
And the earth is painted green,
With such a lot of nice fresh air
All sandwiched in between.

ANONYMOUS

TODAY

So here hath been dawning
    Another blue Day;
Think, wilt thou let it
    Slip useless away?

Out of Eternity
    This new Day is born;
Into Eternity,
    At night, will return.

Behold it aforetime
    No eye ever did;
So soon it forever
    From all eyes is hid.

Here hath been dawning
    Another blue Day;
Then wilt thou let it
    Slip useless away?

THOMAS CARLYLE

THE SINGER

If I had peace to sit and sing,
Then I could make a lovely thing;
But I am stung with goads and whips,
So I build songs like iron ships.

Let it be something for my song.
If it is sometimes swift and strong.

ANNA WICKHAM

TRUTH

Truth, be more precious to me than the eyes
Of happy love; burn hotter in my throat
Than passion, and possess me like my pride;
More sweet than freedom, more desired than joy,
More sacred than the pleasing of a friend.

MAX EASTMAN

THE COIN

Into my heart's treasury
I slipped a coin
That time cannot take
Nor a thief purloin.
Oh, better than the minting
Of a gold-crowned king
Is the safe-kept memory
Of a lovely thing.

SARA TEASDALE

THE HAPPIEST HEART

Who drives the horses of the sun
Shall lord it but a day;
Better the lowly deed were done,
And kept the humble way.

The rust will find the sword of fame,
The dust will hide the crown;
Ay, none shall nail so high his name
Time will not tear it down.

The happiest heart that ever beat
Was in some quiet breast
That found the common daylight sweet,
And left to Heaven the rest.

JOHN VANCE CHENEY

He ate and drank the precious words,
His spirit grew robust;
He knew no more that he was poor,
Nor that his frame was dust.

He danced along the dingy days
And this bequest of wings
Was but a book. What liberty
A loosened spirit brings!

EMILY DICKINSON

MEASURE ME, SKY!

Measure me, sky!
  Tell me I reach by a song
Nearer the stars:
  I have been little so long.

Weigh me, high wind!
  What will your wild scales record?
Profit of pain,
  Joy by the weight of a word.

Horizon, reach out!
  Catch at my hands, stretch them taut,
Rim of the world;
  Widen my eyes by a thought.

Sky, be my depth,
  Wind be my width and my height,
World, my heart's span;
  Loneliness, wings for my flight!

LEONORA SPEYER

GOOD NAME

Good name in man and woman, dear my lord,
Is the immediate jewel of their souls;
Who steals my purse, steals trash; 'tis something, nothing
'Twas mine, 'tis his, and has been slave to thousands;
But he that filches from me my good name,
Robs me of that which not enriches him,
And makes me poor indeed.

WILLIAM SHAKESPEARE

FROM "PRAYER"

From compromise and things half-done,
  Keep me, with stern and stubborn pride.
And when, at last, the fight is won,
  God, keep me still unsatisfied.

LOUIS UNTERMEYER

UP-HILL

Does the road wind up-hill all the way?—
  Yes, to the very end.
Will the day's journey take the whole long day?—
  From morn to night, my friend.

But is there for the night a resting place?
  A roof for when the slow, dark hours begin.
May not the darkness hide it from my face?
  You cannot miss that inn.

Shall I meet other wayfarers at night?
  Those who have gone before.
Then must I knock, or call when just in sight?
  They will not keep you waiting at that door.

Shall I find comfort, travel-sore and weak?
  Of labor you shall find the sum.
Will there be beds for me and all who seek?
  Yea, beds for all who come.

                              CHRISTINA ROSSETTI

LOVE'S LANTERN

Because the road was steep and long
  And through a dark and lonely land,
God set upon my lips a song
  And put a lantern in my hand.

Through miles on weary miles of night
  That stretch endless in my way
My lantern burns serene and white,
  An unexhausted cup of day.

Oh golden lights and lights like wine
  How dim your boasted spendors are!
Behold this little lamp of mine,
  It is more star-like than a star.

                              ALINE KILMER

WHICH

Isn't it strange that princes and kings
And clowns who caper in sawdust rings,
And common folk, like you and me,
Are builders of eternity?

To each is given a bag of tools,
A shapeless mass, a book of rules;
And each must make, ere life has flown,
A stumbling block or a stepping stone.

CALE YOUNG RICE

WORK

Let me but do my work from day to day,
  In field or forest, at the desk or loom,
  In roaring market-place or tranquil room.
Let me but find it in my heart to say,
  When vagrant wishes beckon me astray,
  "This is my work; my blessing, not my doom;
  Of all who live, I am the one by whom
This work can best be done in the right way."

Then shall I see it not too great, nor small
  To suit my spirit and to prove my powers;
Then shall I cheerful greet the labouring hours,
  And cheerful turn, when the long shadows fall
At eventide, to play and love and rest,
  Because I know for me my work is best.

HENRY VAN DYKE

To get at the eternal strength of things
And fearlessly to make strong songs of it,
Is, to my mind, the mission of that man
The world would call a poet. He may sing
But roughly, and withal ungraciously;
But if he touch to life the one right chord
Wherein God's music slumbers, and awake
To truth one drowsed ambition, he sings well.

EDWIN ARLINGTON ROBINSON

ODE

We are the music-makers,
And we are the dreamers of dreams,
Wandering by the lone sea-breakers,
    And sitting by desolate streams;
World-losers and world-forsakers,
    On whom the pale moon gleams;
Yet we are the movers and shakers
    Of the world forever, it seems.

With wonderful deathless ditties
We build up the world's great cities,
    And out of a fabulous story
    We fashion an empire's glory;
One man with a dream, at pleasure,
    Shall go forth and conquer a crown;
And three with a new song's measure
    Can trample an empire down.

We, in the ages lying
In the buried past of the earth,
Built Nineveh with our sighing;
    And Babel itself with our mirth;
And o'erthrew them with prophesying
    To the old of the new world's worth;
For each age is a dream that is dying,
    Or one that is coming to birth.
                ARTHUR WILLIAM EDGAR O'SHAUGHNESSY

We never know how high we are
    Till we are called to rise;
And then, if we are true to plan,
    Our statures touch the skies.

The heroism we recite
    Would be a daily thing,
Did not ourselves the cubits warp
    For fear to be a king.
                EMILY DICKINSON

THE BUILDER

Smoothing a cypress beam
  With a scarred hand,
I saw a carpenter
  In a far land.

Down past the flat roofs
  Poured the white sun;
But still he bent his back,
  The patient one.

And I paused surprised
  In that queer place
To find an old man
  With a haunting face.

"Who art thou, carpenter,
  Of the bowed head;
And what buildest thou?"
  "Heaven," he said.

WILLARD WATTLES

CREEDS

How pitiful are little folk—
They seem so very small;
They look at stars, and think they are
Denominational.

WILLARD WATTLES

He who in his chosen realm of Art
Sings a new song or plants a new tree
Becomes himself a living part
Of Earth's Creative Majesty.

CORA M. DOBSON

RECIPROCITY

I do not think that skies and meadows are
Moral, or that the fixture of a star
Comes of a quiet spirit or that trees
Have wisdom in their windless silences.
Yet these are things invested in my mood
With constancy, and peace, and fortitude,
That in my troubled season I can cry
Upon the wide composure of the sky,
And envy fields, and wish that I might be
As little daunted as a star or tree.

JOHN DRINKWATER

COUNTERSIGN

Out in the dark-night long
I heard the Pine Tree's song
Make secret harmonies
For frozen earth and skies—

And in the first wan light
I watched a grey gull's flight
Toward morning and the sea;
These things did counsel me

To find for Doubt a wing;
To teach Despair to sing;
To make Faith's countersign
A grey Gull and a Pine!

ARTHUR KETCHUM

THE TORCH

Make me a torch for feet that grope
Down Truth's dim trail; to bear for wistful eyes
Comfort of light; to bid great beacons blaze
And kindle altar fires of sacrifice.
Let me set souls aflame with quenchless zeal
For high endeavor; causes true and high—
So would I live to quicken and inspire,
So would I then, consumed, burn out and die.

ALBION FELLOWS BACON

CLAY HILLS

It is easy to mold the yielding clay
And many shapes grow into beauty
Under the facile hand.
But forms of clay are lightly broken;
They will lie shattered and forgotten in a
    dingy corner.

But underneath the slipping clay
Is rock . . .
I would rather work in stubborn rock
All the years of my life,
And make one strong thing
And set it in a high, clean place,
To recall the granite strength of my desire.

JEAN STARR UNTERMEYER

THE LEADEN-EYED

Let not young souls be smothered out before
They do quaint deeds and fully flaunt their pride.
It is the world's one crime its babes grow dull,
Its poor are ox-like, limp and leaden-eyed.

Not that they starve, but starve so dreamlessly,
Not that they sow, but that they seldom reap,
Not that they serve, but have no gods to serve,
Not that they die, but that they die like sheep.

VACHEL LINDSAY

FOUR THINGS

Four things a man must learn to do
If he would make his record true;
To think without confusion clearly;
To love his fellow-men sincerely;
To act from honest motives purely;
To trust in God and Heaven securely.

HENRY VAN DYKE

MY WAGE

I bargained with Life for a penny,
   And Life would pay no more,
However I begged at evening
   When I counted my scanty store;

For Life is a just employer,
   He gives you what you ask,
But once you have set the wages,
   Why, you must bear the task.

I worked for a menial's hire,
   Only to learn, dismayed,
That any wage I had asked of Life,
   Life would have paid.

JESSIE B. RITTENHOUSE

MAN-MAKING

We all are blind until we see
   That in the human plan
Nothing is worth the making if
   It does not make the man.

Why build these cities glorious
   If man unbuilded goes?
In vain we build the world, unless
   The builder also grows.

EDWIN MARKHAM

STANDARDS

White is the skimming gull on the sombre green of the fir-trees,
Black is the soaring gull on a snowy glimmer of cloud.

CHARLES WHARTON STORK

OPPORTUNITY

They do me wrong who say I come no more
   When once I knock and fail to find you in;
For every day I stand outside your door
   And bid you wake and rise to fight and win;

Wail not for precious chances passed away!
   Weep not for golden ages on the wane!
Each night I burn the records of the day—
   At sunrise every soul is born again.

                                    WALTER MALONE

MUSIC I HEARD

Music I heard with you was more than music,
   And bread I broke with you was more than bread,
Now that I am without you, all is desolate,
   All that was once so beautiful is dead.

Your hands once touched this table and this silver,
   And I have seen your fingers hold this glass.
These things do not remember you, beloved:
   And yet your touch upon them will not pass.

For it was in my heart you moved among them,
   And blessed them with your hands and with your eyes.
   And in my heart they will remember always:
   They knew you once, O beautiful and wise!

                                    CONRAD AIKEN

PRIMER LESSON

Look out how you use proud words.
When you let proud words go, it is not easy
      to call them back.
They wear long boots, hard boots; they walk off proud;
      they can't hear you calling—
Look out how you use proud words.

                                    CARL SANDBERG

THE BUILDER

How great will be the thing that he builds?
  Not quite so great as his dreams are great;
Not quite so high as his hopes are high;
  And long he must build and wait.
But the glory is, if he builds what he can,
That all the while he is building a Man!

And what will he build as the years go by,
  With stone or steel or the might of a theme?
No mansion, we know, can he ever build
  Out of a cottage dream.
But the glory is, if he builds at all,
That his soul can look o'er the highest wall!

GLENN WARD DRESBACH

THE NATION'S BUILDERS

Not gold, but only men can make
A people great and strong—
Men who, for truth and honor's sake,
Stand fast and suffer long.

Brave men, who work while others sleep
Who dare while others fly—
They build a nation's pillars deep
And lift them to the sky.

RALPH WALDO EMERSON

THE RAINBOW

My heart leaps up when I behold
A rainbow in the sky:
So was it when my life began;
So is it now I am a man:
So be it when I shall grow old,
    Or let me die!
The Child is father of the Man
And I could wish my days to be
Bound each to each by natural piety.

WILLIAM WORDSWORTH

WHAT IS GOOD?

"What is the real good?"
I asked in musing mood.

Order, said the law court;
Knowledge, said the school;
Truth, said the wise man;
Pleasure, said the fool;
Love, said the maiden;
Beauty, said the page;
Freedom, said the dreamer;
Home, said the sage;
Fame, said the soldier;
Equity, the seer—

Spake my heart full sadly,
"The answer is not here."

Then within my bosom
Softly this I heard:
"Each heart holds the secret;
Kindness is the word."

JOHN BOYLE O'REILLY

"NOW HOLLOW FIRES BURN OUT TO BLACK"

Now hollow fires burn out to black,
And lights are guttering low:
Square your shoulders, lift your pack,
And leave your friends and go.

Oh never fear, man, nought's to dread,
Look not to left nor right:
In all the endless road you tread
There's nothing but the night.

A. E. HOUSMAN

Who seeks for heaven alone to save his soul
May keep the path, but will not reach the goal;
While he who walks in love may wander far,
But God will bring him where the blessed are.

HENRY VAN DYKE

EACH IN HIS OWN TONGUE

A Fire-mist and a planet—
 A crystal and a cell,—
A jelly-fish and a saurian,
 And caves where the cave-men dwell;
Then a sense of law and beauty,
 And a face turned from the clod,—
Some call it Evolution,
 And others call it God.

A haze on the far horizon,
 The infinite, tender sky,
The ripe, rich tints of the cornfields,
 And the wild geese circling high,—
And all over upland and lowland
 The charm of the goldenrod,—
Some of us call it Autumn,
 And others call it God.

Like tides on a crescent sea-beach,
 When the moon is new and thin,
Into our hearts high yearnings
 Come welling and surging in,—
Come from the distant ocean
 Whose rim no foot has trod,—
Some of us call it Longing,
 And others call it God.

A picket frozen on duty,—
 A mother starved for her brood,—
Socrates drinking the hemlock,
 And Jesus on the rood;
And millions who, humble and nameless,
 The straight, hard pathway plod,—
Some call it Consecration,
 And others call it God.

WILLIAM HERBERT CARRUTH

THE FIRES

Men make them fires on the hearth
    Each under his roof-tree,
And the Four Winds that rule the earth
    They blow the smoke to me.

Across the high hills and the sea
    And all the changeful skies,
The Four Winds blow the smoke to me
    Till the tears are in my eyes.

Until the tears are in my eyes
    And my heart is wellnigh broke
For thinking on old memories
    That gather in the smoke.

With every shift of every wind
    The homesick memories come,
From every quarter of mankind
    Where I have made me a home.

Four times a fire against the cold
    And a roof against the rain—
Sorrow fourfold and joy fourfold
    The Four Winds bring again!

How can I answer which is best
    Of all the fires that burn?
I have been too often host or guest
    At every fire in turn.

How can I turn from any fire,
    Or any man's hearthstone?
I know the wonder and desire
    That went to build my own!

How can I doubt man's joy or woe
    Where'er his house-fires shine,
Since all that man must undergo
    Will visit me at mine?

Oh, you Four Winds that blow so strong
  And know that this is true,
Stoop for a little and carry my song
  To all the men I knew!

Where there are fires against the cold,
  Or roofs against the rain—
With love fourfold and joy fourfold,
  Take them my songs again!

RUDYARD KIPLING

A PRAYER

Give me work to do;
Give me health;
Give me joy in simple things.
Give me an eye for beauty,
A tongue for truth,
A heart that loves,
A mind that reasons,
A sympathy that understands;
Give me neither malice nor envy,
But a true kindness
And a noble common sense.
At the close of each day
Give me a book,
And a friend with whom
I can be silent.

AUTHOR UNKOWN

THE HEART THAT DARES

Oh the stirring and rough and impetuous song—
The song of the heart that dares,
That keeps to its creed and gives no heed
To the faces that fortune wears.

That heart that laughs when the foe is met,
And thrives and fires at taunt and threat,
And finds no toiling and traveling long,
For the sake of the good it bears.

UNKNOWN

She sweeps with many-colored brooms,
And leaves the shreds behind;
Oh, housewife in the evening west,
Come back, and dust the pond!

You dropped a purple ravelling in,
You dropped an amber thread;
And now you've littered all the East
With duds of emerald!

And still she plies her spotted broom,
And still the aprons fly,
Till brooms fade softly into stars—
And then I come away.

EMILY DICKINSON

ROMANCE

I will make you brooches and toys for your delight
Of bird-song at morning and star-shine at night.
I will make a palace fit for you and me,
Of green days in forests and blue days at sea.

I will make my kitchen, and you shall keep your room,
Where white flows the river and bright blows the broom,
And you shall wash your linen and keep your body white
In rainfall at morning and dewfall at night.

And this shall be for music when no one else is near
The fine song for singing, the rare song to hear!
That only I remember, that only you admire,
Of the broad road that stretches and the roadside fire.

ROBERT LOUIS STEVENSON

FATE

Two shall be born the whole wide world apart;
And speak in different tongues, and have no thought
Each of the other's being, and no heed;
And these o'er unknown seas to unknown lands
Shall cross, escaping wreck, defying death,
And all unconsciously shape every act
And bend each wandering step to this one end,
That, one day, out of darkness, they shall meet
And read life's meaning in each other's eyes.

And two shall walk some narrow way of life
So nearly side by side, that should one turn
Ever so little space to left or right
They needs must stand acknowledged face to face.
And yet, with wistful eyes that never meet,
With groping hands that never clasp, and lips
Calling in vain to ears that never hear,
They seek each other all their weary days
And die unsatisfied—and all this is Fate.

SUSAN MARR SPALDING

MENDING WALL

Something there is that doesn't love a wall,
That sends the frozen-ground-swell under it,
And spills the upper boulders in the sun;
And makes gaps even two can pass abreast.
The work of hunters is another thing:
I have come after them and make repair
Where they have left not one stone on a stone,
But they would have the rabbit out of hiding,
To please the yelping dogs. The gaps I mean,
No one has seen them made or heard them made,
But at spring mending-time we find them there.
I let my neighbor know beyond the hill;
And on a day we meet to walk the line
And set the wall between us once again.
We keep the wall between us as we go.
To each the boulders that have fallen to each.
And some are loaves and some so nearly balls
We have to use a spell to make them balance:
"Stay where you are until our backs are turned!"
We wear our fingers rought with handling them.
Oh, just another kind of outdoor game,
One on a side. It comes to little more:
There where it is we do not need the wall:
He is all pine and I am apple-orchard.
My apple trees will never get across
And eat the cones under his pines, I tell him.
He only says, "Good fences make good neighbors."
Spring is the mischief in me, and I wonder
If I could put a notion in his head:
"Why do they make good neighbors? Isn't it
Where there are cows? But here there are no cows.

Before I built a wall I'd ask to know
What I was walling in or walling out,
And to whom I was like to give offense.
Something there is that doesn't love a wall,
That wants it down!'' I could say ''elves'' to him,
But it's not elves exactly, and I'd rather
He said it for himself. I see him there,
Bringing a stone grasped firmly by the top
In each hand, like an old-stone savage armed.
He moves in darkness, as it seems to me,
Not of woods only and the shade of trees.
He will not go behind his father's saying,
And he likes having thought of it so well
He says again, ''Good fences make good neighbors.''

ROBERT FROST

THE DIVINE STRATEGY

No soul can be forever banned,
    Eternally bereft;
Whoever falls from God's right hand
    Is caught into His left.

EDWIN MARKHAM

WINDOWS

I looked through other's windows
    On an enchanted earth,
But out of my own window—
    Solitude and dearth.

And yet there is a mystery
    I cannot understand—
That others through my window
    See an enchanted land.

JESSIE B. RITTENHOUSE

AN IMMORALITY

Sing we for love and idleness,
Naught else is worth the having.

Though I have been in many a land,
There is naught else in living.

And I would rather have my sweet,
Though rose-leaves die of grieving,

Than do high deeds in Hungary
To pass all men's believing.

EZRA POUND

ROMANY GOLD

There's a crackle of brown on the leaf's crisp edge
And the goldenrod blooms have begun to feather.
We're two jolly vagabonds under a hedge
By the dusty road together.

Could an emperor boast such a house as ours,
The sky for a roof and for couch the clover?
Does he sleep as well under silken flowers
As we, when the day is over?

He sits at ease at his table fine
With the richest of meat and drink before him.
I eat my crust with your hand in mine,
And your eyes are cups of a stronger wine
Than any his steward can pour him.

What if the autumn days grow cold?
Under one cloak we can brave the weather.
A comrade's troth is the Romany gold,
And we're taking the road together.

AMELIA JOSEPHINE BURR

BROTHERHOOD

Of all things beautiful and good,
The kingliest is brotherhood;
For it will bring again to earth
Her long-lost poesy and mirth;
And till it comes these men are slaves,
And travel downward to the dust of graves.

Clear the way, then, clear the way;
Blind creeds and kings have had their day.
Break the dead branches from the path;
Our hope is in the aftermath,
To this event the ages ran:
Make way for brotherhood—make way for man.

EDWIN MARKHAM

OUTWITTED

He drew a circle that shut me out—
Heretic, rebel, a thing to flout.
But love and I had the wit to win:
We drew a circle and took him in!

EDWIN MARKHAM

WONDER

So intimate with joy was I,
    So rich in splendid dreams,
So friendly with the hills, the sky,
    The trees, the living streams,
That I was fain to share in part
    The joy that I had known,
But found in many a quiet heart
    Dreams fairer than my own!

NANCY BUCKLEY

SONG

Love's on the highroad,
Love's in the byroad;
Love's on the meadow and
Love's in the mart!
And down every byway
Where I've taken my way,
I've met Love a-smiling for
Love's in my heart.

DANA BURNET

THE NIGHT HAS A THOUSAND EYES

The night has a thousand eyes,
And the day but one;
Yet the light of the bright world dies
With the dying sun.

The mind has a thousand eyes,
And the heart but one;
Yet the light of a whole life dies
When love is done.

FRANCIS WILLIAM BOURDILLON

PRAYER

It is my joy in life to find
At every turning of the road,
The strong arm of a comrade kind
To help me onward with my load.

And since I have no gold to give,
And love alone must make amends,
My only prayer is, while I live,
God, make me worthy of my friends!

FRANK DEMPSTER SHERMAN

A CREED

There is a destiny that makes us brothers,
 None goes his way alone;
All that we send into the lives of others
 Comes back into our own.

I care not what his temple or his creed,
 One thing holds firm and fast—
That into his fateful heap of days and deeds
 The soul of a man is cast.

EDWIN MARKHAM

BLIND

The Spring blew trumpets of colors;
 Her Green sang in my brain—
I heard a blind man groping,
 "Tap-tap" with his cane.

I pitied him in his blindness;
 But can I boast, "I see"?
Perhaps there walks a spirit
 Close by, who pities me—

A spirit who hears me tapping,
 The five-sensed cane of mind,
Amid such unguessed glories—
 That I am worse than blind.

HARRY KEMP

SONG

Love that is hoarded, moulds at last
 Until we know some day
The only thing we ever have
 Is what we give away.

And kindness that is never used
 But hidden all alone
Will slowly harden till it is
 As hard as any stone.

It is the things we always hold
 That we will lose some day;
The only things we ever keep
 Are what we give away.

LOUIS GINSBERG

THE HUMAN TOUCH

High thoughts and noble in all lands
Help me; my soul is fed by such.
But ah, the touch of lips and hands,—
The human touch!
Warm, vital, close, life's symbols dear,—
These need I most, and now, and here.

RICHARD BURTON

TO ANY ONE

Whether the time be slow or fast,
    Enemies, hand in hand,
Must come together at the last
    And understand.

No matter how the die is cast,
    Nor who may seem to win,
You know that you must love at last—
    Why not begin?

WITTER BYNNER

LOVE'S ISLAND
(From the Japanese of Doku-ho)

An island in an island sea;
    "Too small for me!" I sadly cried.
And then espied
A lark that rose into the sky.
Whereat, I changed my plaintive cry;
    "If lark there be
    Then field there is.
    If field there be,
    Then man there is.
    If man there be
    Then Love there is.
Then large enough, indeed, for me,
Thou little island in the sea!"

IAN OLIVER

SOULS

My Soul goes clad in gorgeous things,
　Scarlet and gold and blue;
And at her shoulder sudden wings
　Like long flames flicker through.

And she is swallow-fleet and free
　From mortal bonds and bars.
She laughs, because eternity
　Blossoms for her with stars!

O folk who scorn my stiff gray gown,
　My dull and foolish face,—
Can ye not see my Soul flash down,
　A singing flame through space?

And folk, whose earth-stained looks I hate,
　Why may I not divine
Your souls, that must be passionate,
　Shining and swift, as mine?

FANNIE STEARNS DAVIS

ABOU BEN ADHEM

Abou Ben Adhem (may his tribe increase!)
Awoke one night from a dream of peace,
And saw within the moonlight in his room,
Making it rich and like a lily in bloom,
An angel writing in a book of gold:
Exceeding peace had made Ben Adhem bold,
And to the presence in the room he said,
"What writest thou?"—The vision raised its head,
And, with a look made all of sweet accord,
Answered, "The names of those who love the Lord."
"And is mine one?" said Abou; "Nay, not so,"
Replied the angel. Abou spoke more low,
But cheerly still; and said, "I pray, thee, then,
Write me as one that loves his fellow-men."
The angel wrote, and vanished. The next night
It came again, with a great 'wakening light,
And showed the names whom love of God had Blessed—
And Lo! Ben Adhem's led all the rest!

LEIGH HUNT

A CLEAR NIGHT

I have worn this day as a fretting, ill-made garment,
Impatient to be rid of it;
And lo, as I drew it off over my shoulders
This jewel caught in my hair.

KARLE WILSON BAKER

"WITH RUE MY HEART IS LADEN"

With rue my heart is laden
  For golden friends I had,
For many a rose-lipt maiden
  And many a lightfoot lad.

By brooks too broad for leaping
  The lightfoot boys are laid;
The rose-lipt girls are sleeping
  In fields where roses fade.

A. E. HOUSMAN

CONVERSATIONS

Last night we talked of certain mysteries
  As strange and lovely as the rising moon:
Of beauty, wisdom, old philosophies,
  Of sorrow that finds every man so soon,
Of love and laughter, sunlight on a hill,
  The way a little wind has with the grass,
Of souls that dream and dreams that linger still
  Though men and ages like the sunshine pass.

We met this morning quite a chance affair.
  You cannot see of course into my brain,
You do not know the nights that flourish there.
  You said, "It's rather warmer since the rain."
And getting my profoundest thoughts together
  I answered, "Yes, it's like September weather."

MIRIAM VEDDER

CHARTLESS

I never saw a moor,
  I never saw the sea;
Yet now I know how heather looks,
  And what a wave must be.

I never spoke with God,
  Nor visited in Heaven:
Yet certain am I of the spot
  As if the chart were given.

EMILY DICKINSON

FRIENDS

My friends have been like daily bread,
Essential yet unmerited,
As kind as sunshine after rain
And firelight on the window pane;
As kind as harbor lights at sea
Or some familiar melody;
As good as salt my friends to me.

W. LETTS

CONTRASTS

The people whom I love the best
Are never here but East, or West;
And those from whom I'd run away
I always see them every day.

The things I love to talk about
My heart will seldom let them out;
For folks I see prefer to hear
About the weathers of the year.

But Oh the places I would find!
The people that I'd leave behind!
While just the few that went with me
Related to my heart should be.

E. T. WOODWORTH

FRIENDSHIP

If Thought unlock her mysteries,
  If Friendship on me smile,
I walk in marble galleries,
  I talk with kings the while.

RALPH WALDO EMERSON

HUMILITY

Humble we must be
  If to Heaven we go.
High is the roof there,
  But the gate is low.

ROBERT HERRICK

O! Many a shaft at random sent,
Finds mark the archer little meant,
And many a word, at random spoken,
May soothe or wound a heart that's broken!

SIR WALTER SCOTT

MY WIFE

Trusty, dusky, vivid, true,
With eyes of gold and bramble-dew,
  Steel-true and blade-straight,
The great artificer
  Made my mate.

Honour, anger, valour, fire;
A love that life could never tire,
  Death quench or evil stir,
The mighty master
  Gave to her.

Teacher, tender, comrade, wife,
A fellow-farer true through life,
  Heart-whole and soul-free
The august father
  Gave to me.

ROBERT LOUIS STEVENSON

ARIEL'S SONG

Where the bee sucks, there suck I;
In a cowslip's bell I lie;
There I couch when owls do cry;
On the bat's back I do fly
After summer merrily.
Merrily, merrily shall I live now,
Under the blossom that hangs on the bough.

WILLIAM SHAKESPEARE

"Not what we give, but what we share—
For the gift without the giver is bare.
Who gives himself with his alms feeds three,
Himself, his hungering neighbor, and me."

From the Vision of Sir Launfal
JAMES RUSSELL LOWELL

THE VENTURE

I never see a map but I'm away
On all the errands that I long to do,
Up all the rivers that are painted blue,
And all the ranges that are painted gray,
And into those pale places where they say:
"Unknown." Oh, what they never knew
I would be knowing—were it not for you
I would be off tomorrow with the day!
Then, since I am at anchor at your door,
Befriend the wistful stranger; make me free
Of all your little country and its store
Of unknown things and wonders—spread for me
The charts and let me venture, till I find
The secrets of your beauty and your mind.

JEAN KENYON MACKENZIE

SONG OF THE OPEN ROAD

Afoot and light-hearted, I take to the open road,
Healthy, free, the world before me,
The long brown path before me, leading wherever
I choose.

Henceforth I ask not good fortune—I myself am
good fortune;
Henceforth I whimper no more, postpone no more,
need nothing,
Strong and content, I travel the open road.

From "The Song of the Open Road"
WALT WHITMAN

THE WORLD'S NEED

So many gods, so many creeds,
So many paths that wind and wind,
While just the art of being kind
Is all this sad world needs.
ELLA WHEELER WILCOX

MORNING SONG

There's a mellower light just over the hill,
And somewhere a yellower daffodil,
And honey, somewhere, that's sweeter still.

And some were meant to stay like a stone,
Knowing the things they have always known,
Sinking down deeper into their own.

But some must follow the wind and me,
Who like to be starting and like to be free,
Never so glad as we're going to be!
KARLE WILSON BAKER

THE WORLD'S WANDERERS

Tell me, thou star, whose wings of light
Speed thee in thy fiery flight,
In what cavern of the night
   Will thy pinions close now?

Tell me, moon, thou pale and gray
Pilgrim of heaven's homeless way,
In what depth of night or day
   Seekest thou repose now?

Weary wind, who wanderest
Like the world's rejected guest
Hast thou still some secret nest
   On the tree or billow?

PERCY BYSSHE SHELLEY

THE GOLDEN SHOES

The winds are lashing on the sea;
   The roads are blind with storm
And it's far and far away with me;
   So bide you there, stay warm.
It's forth I must, and forth today;
   And I have no path to choose.
The highway hill, it is my way still.
   Give me my golden shoes.

God gave them me on that first day
   I knew that I was young.
And I looked forth, from west to north;
   And I heard the Songs unsung.

This cloak is worn too threadbare thin,
  But ah, how weatherwise!
This girdle serves to bind it in;
  What heed of wondering eyes?—
And yet beside, I wear one pride
  —Too bright, you think, to use?—
That I must wear, and still keep fair,—
  Give me my golden shoes.

God gave them me on that first day
  I heard the stars all chime.
And I looked forth far, from road to star;
  And I knew it was far to climb.

They would buy me house and hearth, no doubt,
  And the mirth to spend and share;
Could I sell that gift, and go without,
  Or wear—what neighbors wear.
But take my staff, my purse, my scrip;
  For I have one thing to choose.
For you,—Godspeed! May you soothe your need.
  For me, my golden shoes!

He gave them me, that far, first day
  When I heard all songs unsung.
And I looked far forth, from west to north.
  God saw that I was young!

                JOSEPHINE PRESTON PEABODY

ADVENTURE

Sun and wind and beat of sea,
Great lands stretching endlessly . . .
Where be bonds to bind the free?
All the world was made for me!

                ADELAIDE CRAPSEY

THE ROAD NOT TAKEN

Two roads diverged in a yellow wood,
    And sorry I could not travel both
And be one traveller, long I stood
And looked down one as far as I could
    To where it bent in the undergrowth;

Then took the other, as just as fair,
    And having perhaps the better claim,
Because it was grassy and wanted wear;
Though as for that the passing there
    Had worn them really about the same,

And both that morning equally lay
    In leaves no step had trodden black.
Oh, I kept the first for another day!
Yet knowing how way leads on to way,
    I doubted if I should ever come back.

I shall be telling this with a sigh
    Somewhere ages and ages hence;
Two roads diverged in a wood, and I—
I took the one less travelled by,
    And that has made all the difference.

ROBERT FROST

THE WANDERER

The ships are lying in the bay,
    The gulls are swinging 'round their spars;
My soul as eagerly as they
    Desires the margin of the stars.

So much do I love wandering,
    So much I love the sea and sky,
That it will be a piteous thing
    In one small grave to lie.

ZOE AKINS

FROM "THE JOYS OF THE ROAD"

Now the joys of the road are chiefly these:
A crimson touch on the hard-wood trees;

A vagrant's morning wide and blue,
In early fall, when the wind walks, too;

A shadowy highway cool and brown,
Alluring up and enticing down

From rippled water to dappled swamp,
From purple glory to scarlet pomp;

The outward eye, the quiet will,
And the striding heart from hill to hill;

The tempter apple over the fence;
The cobweb bloom on the yellow quince;

The palish asters along the wood,—
A lyric touch in the solitude;

An open hand, an easy shoe,
And a hope to make the day go through,—

Another to sleep with, and a third
To wake me up at the voice of a bird;

The resonant far-listening morn,
And the hoarse whisper of the corn;

The crickets mourning their comrades lost,
In the night's retreat from the gathering frost;

(Or is it their slogan, plaintive and shrill,
As they beat on their corselets, valiant still?)
• • •
An idle noon, a bubbling spring,
The seas in the pine-tops murmuring;
• • •
And O the joy that is never won,
But follows and follows the journeying sun

By marsh and tide, by meadow and stream,
A will-o-'the-wind, a light-o'-dream,

The racy smell of the forest loam,
When stealthy, sad-heart leaves go home;

(O leaves, O leaves, I am one with you,
Of the mould and the sun and the wind
    and the dew.)

The broad gold wake of the afternoon;
The silent fleck of the old new moon;

The sound of the hollow sea's release
From stormy tumult to starry peace;
                • • •
These are the joys of the open road—
For him who travels without a load.

                                    BLISS CARMAN

THE HOUSE AND THE ROAD

The little Road says, Go;
    The little House says, Stay:
And O, it's bonny here at home,
    But I must go away.

The little Road, like me,
    Would seek and turn and know;
And forth I must, to learn the things
    The little Road would show!

And go I must, my dears,
    And journey while I may,
Though heart be sore for the little House
    That had no word but Stay.

Maybe, no other way
    Your child could ever know
Why a little House would have you stay,
    When a little Road says, Go.

                        JOSEPHINE PRESTON PEABODY

THE WANDERER

Whose farthest footsteps never strayed
   Beyond the village of his birth
Is but a lodger for the night
   In this old wayside inn of earth.

Tomorrow he shall take his pack
   And set out for the ways beyond
On the old trail from star to star,
   An alien and a vagabond.

               RICHARD HOVEY

CANOE TRAILS

Broad is the track that the steamer takes,
   Over the open sea,
Wide are the waves of the windy lake,
   Dear are the lakes to me,
And the sparkling sound is good,
Bright is the river, too,
But the stream that winds to the heart of the woods
Is the trail of the little canoe.

Dip of the paddles, gurgle and splash,
   Quiet and bird-note clear,
White of the birch, grey of the ash—
   Balm of the heart is here.
Here where the bolder footpaths cease,
Here where the best is true,
The loveliest road to the shrines of peace
Is the trail of the little canoe.

               ARTHUR GUITERMAN

A CAMP

The bed was made, the room was fit,
By punctual eve the stars were lit;
The air was still, the water ran,
No need was there for maid or man,
When we put up, my ass and I,
At God's green caravanserai.

               ROBERT LOUIS STEVENSON

Let us go in once more
By some blue mountain door
And hold communion with the forest leaves.

BLISS CARMAN

HIGHWAYS

Who's learned the lure of trodden ways
   And walked them up and down,
May love a steeple in a mist,
   But cannot love a town.

Who's worn a bit of purple once
   Can never, never lie
All smothered in a little box
   When stars are in the sky.

· · ·

Who's ground the grist of trodden ways—
   The gray dust and the brown—
May love red tiling two miles off,
   But cannot love a town.

LESLIE NELSON JENNINGS

FROM A RAILWAY CARRIAGE

Faster than fairies, faster than witches,
Bridges and houses, hedges and ditches;
And charging along like troops in a battle,
All through the meadows the horses and cattle:
All of the sights of the hill and the plain
Fly as thick as driving rain;
And ever again, in the wink of an eye,
Painted stations whistle by.

Here is a child who clambers and scrambles,
All by himself and gathering brambles;
Here is a tramp who stands and gazes;
And there is the green for stringing the daisies!
Here is a cart run away in the road
Lumping along with man and load;
And here is a mill, and there is a river:
Each a glimpse and gone for ever!

ROBERT LOUIS STEVENSON

WIND-IN-THE-HAIR AND RAIN-IN-THE-FACE

Wind-in-the-hair and Rain-in-the-face
Are friends worth the having, and yours to command;
For many's the hour and many's the place
We've frolicked together on ocean and land.

They'll brighten the darks of your gloomiest mood!
They'll strengthen your heart with their boisterous play,
They'll buffet your anger until it's subdued,
They'll sport with your sorrow and whisk it away.

Don't clutch at your curls with that grasp of despair!
A tear on the cheek is a drop out of place!
"I'll rumple your tresses!" roars Wind-in-the-hair.
"Let me do your crying!" trills Rain-in-the-face.

No seven-league boots like a pair of old shoes,
No wish-cloak that equals a rain-beaded coat,
To take you away from the Realm of the Blues,
To give you the will that grips Care by the throat!

How petty our griefs under God's open sky!
How often but ghosts of a conjuring brain!
How quickly they dwindle, how lightly they fly,
When winnowed and washed by the rain!

Then on with your shabbiest, hardiest wear!
(The kind that the women folk term "a disgrace!")
And swing down the highway with Wind-in-the hair,
Or splash through the puddles with Rain-in-the-face!

ARTHUR GUITERMAN

FRIENDSHIP

Unbar the door, since thou the Opener art,
   Show me the forward way, since thou art
     guide,
I put no faith in pilot or in chart,
   Since they are transient, and thou dost
     abide.

RALPH WALDO EMERSON

A VAGABOND SONG

There is something in the Autumn that is native to my blood—
Touch of manner, hint of mood;
And my heart is like a rhyme,
With the yellow and the purple and the crimson keeping time.

The scarlet of the maples can shake me like the cry
Of bugles going by.
And my lonely spirit thrills
To see the frosty asters like a smoke upon the hills.

There is something in October sets the gypsy blood astir;
We must rise and follow her,
When from every hill of flame
She calls and calls each vagabond by name.

BLISS CARMAN

FROM "THE ROAD TO VAGABONDIA"

Oh, to walk the road at morning, when the wind is blowing clean,
And the yellow daisies fling their gold across a world of green—
For the wind it heals the heartache, and the sun it dries the scars,
On the road to Vagabondia that lies beneath the stars.

'Twas the wonder of our going cast a spell about our feet—
And we walked because the world was young, because the way was
    sweet;
And we slept in wild-rose meadows by the little wayside farms,
Till the Dawn came up the highroad with the dead moon in her
    arms.

Oh, the Dawn it went before us through a shining lane of skies,
And the Dream was at our heartstrings, and the light was in our
    eyes,
And we made no boasts of glory and we made no boast of birth,
On the road to Vagabondia that lies across the earth!

DANA BURNET

WORLD-STRANGENESS

Strange the world about me lies,
   Never yet familiar grown—
Still disturbs me with surprise,
   Haunts me like a face half known.

In this house with starry dome,
   Floored with gemlike plains and seas,
Shall I never feel at home,
   Never wholly be at ease?

On from room to room I stray,
   Yet my Host can ne'er espy,
And I know not to this day
   Whether guest or captive I.

So, between the starry dome
   And the floor of plains and seas,
I have never felt at home,
   Never wholly been at ease.

                 WILLIAM WATSON

HIE AWAY

Hie away, hie away!
Over bank and over brae,
Where the copsewood is the greenest,
Where the fountains glisten sheenest,
Where the lady fern grows strongest,
Where the morning dew lies longest,
Where the blackcock sweetest sips it,
Where the fairy latest trips it:
Hie to haunts right seldom seen,
Lovely, lonesome, cool and green,
   Over bank and over brae,
Hie away, hie away!

                 SIR WALTER SCOTT

ROOFS

The road is wide and the stars are out and the breath of the night
  is sweet,
And this is the time when Wanderlust should seize upon my feet.
But I'm glad to turn from the open road and the starlight on my
  face
And leave the splendor of out-of-doors for a human dwelling-place.

I never have known a vagabond who really liked to roam
All up and down the streets of the world and never have a home.
The tramp who slept in your barn last night and left at break of
  day
Will wander only until he finds another place to stay.

The gypsy-man sleeps in his cart with canvas overhead,
Or else he crawls into a tent when it is time for bed.
He will take his ease upon the grass so long as the sun is high
But when it is dark he wants a roof to keep away the sky.

If you call the gypsy a vagabond I think you do him wrong,
For he never goes a-traveling but he takes his home along;
And the only reason a road is good, as every wanderer knows,
Is just because of the homes, the homes, the homes to which it goes!

They say life is a highway and its milestones are the years,
And now and then there's a toll-gate where you pay your way with
  tears.
It's a rough road and a steep road and it stretches broad and far
But it leads at last to a Golden Town where golden houses are.

JOYCE KILMER

I have come from the spring woods,
From the fragrant solitudes;
Listen what the poplar tree,
And murmuring waters counselled me.

RALPH WALDO EMERSON

A TOWN WINDOW

Beyond my window in the night
  Is but a drab inglorious street,
Yet there the frost and clean starlight
  As over Warwick woods are sweet.

Under the grey drift of the town
  The crocus works among the mould
As eagerly as those that crown
  The Warwick spring in flame and gold.

And when the tramway down the hill
  Across the cobbles moans and rings,
There is about my window-sill
  The tumult of a thousand wings.

JOHN DRINKWATER

"INTO MY HEART AN AIR THAT KILLS"

Into my heart an air that kills
  From yon far country blows:
What are those blue remembered hills,
  What spires, what farms are those?

That is the land of lost content,
  I see it shining plain,
The happy highways where I went
  And cannot come again.

A. E. HOUSMAN

SPRING

Now that the winter's gone, the earth hath lost
Her snow-white robes; and now no more the frost
Candies the grass or casts an icy cream
Upon the silver lake or crystal stream:
But the warm sun thaws the benumbed earth,
And makes it tender; gives a sacred birth
To the dead swallow; wakes in hollow tree
The drowsy cuckoo and the bumble-bee.
Now do a choir of chirping minstrels bring
In triumph to the world the youthful spring!
The valleys, hills, and woods, in rich array,
Welcome the coming of the longed-for May.

THOMAS HARDY

A WANDERER'S SONG

A wind's in the heart of me, a fire's in my heels,
I am tired of brick and stone and rumbling wagon-wheels;
I hunger for the sea's edge, the limits of the land,
Where the wild old Atlantic is shouting on the sand.

Oh, I'll be going, leaving the noises of the street,
Go where a lifting foresail-foot is yanking at the sheet;
To a windy, tossing anchorage where yawls and ketches ride,
Oh, I'll be going, going, until I meet the tide.

And first I'll hear the sea-wind, the mewing of the gulls,
The clucking, sucking of the sea about the rusty hulls,
The songs at the capstan in the hooker warping out,
And then the heart of me'll know I'm there or thereabout.

Oh, I am tired of brick and stone, the heart of me is sick,
For windy green, unquiet sea, the realm of Moby Dick;
And I'll be going, going, from the roaring of the wheels,
For a wind's in the heart of me, a fire's in my heels.

JOHN MASEFIELD

SYMBOL

My faith is all a doubtful thing,
  Woven on a doubtful loom,—
Until there comes, each showery spring,
  A cherry-tree in bloom;

And Christ Who died upon a tree
  That death had stricken bare,
Comes beautifully back to me,
  In blossoms, everywhere.

DAVID MORTON

SWEET SEPTEMBER

O sweet September! thy first breezes bring
  The dry leaf's rustle and the squirrel's laughter,
The cool, fresh air, whence health and vigor spring,
  And promise of exceeding joy hereafter.

GEORGE ARNOLD

HOME THOUGHTS FROM EUROPE

'Tis fine to see the Old World, and travel up and down
Among the famous palaces and cities of renown,
To admire the crumbly castles and the statues of the kings,—
But now I think I've had enough of antiquated things.

So it's home again, and home again, America for me!
My heart is turning home again, and there I long to be,
In the land of youth and freedom beyond the ocean bars,
Where the air is full of sunlight and the flag is full of stars.

Oh, London is a man's town, there's power in the air;
And Paris is a woman's town, with flowers in her hair;
And it's sweet to dream in Venice, and it's great to study Rome;
But when it comes to living, there is no place like Home.

I like the German fir-woods, in green battalions drilled;
I like the gardens of Versailles with flashing fountains filled;
But oh, to take your hand, my dear, and ramble for a day
In the friendly western woodland where Nature has her way!

I know that Europe's wonderful, yet something seems to lack;
The Past is too much with her, and the people looking back,
But the glory of the Present is to make the Future free,—
We love our land for what she is and what she is to be.

Oh, it's home again, and home again, America for me!
I want a ship that's westward bound to plough the rolling sea
To the blessed land of Room Enough beyond the ocean bars,
Where the air is full of sunlight and the flag is full of stars.

HENRY VAN DYKE

EASTER

The air is like a butterfly
  With frail blue wings,
The happy earth looks at the sky
  And sings.

JOYCE KILMER

FROM "THE LADY OF SHALOTT"

On either side the river lie
Long fields of barley and of rye,
That clothe the wold and meet the sky;
And through the field the road runs by
    To many-towered Camelot;
And up and down the people go,
Gazing where the lilies blow
'Round an island there below,
    The Island of Shalott.

Willows whiten, aspens quiver,
Little breezes dusk and shiver
Through the wave that runs forever
By the island of the river
    Flowing down to Camelot.
Four gray walls, and four gray towers,
    Overlook a space of flowers
And the silent isle embowers
    The Lady of Shalott.

ALFRED TENNYSON

MY NATIVE LAND

Breathes there a man with soul so dead,
Who never to himself hath said,
"This is my own—my native land!"
Whose heart hath ne'er within him burned,
As home his footsteps he hath turned,
From wandering on a foreign strand?
If such there breathe, go, mark him well!
For him no minstrel's raptures swell.
High though his titles, proud his name,
Boundless his wealth as wish can claim,—
Despite those titles, power, and pelf,
The wretch, concentered all in self,
Living shall forfeit fair renown,
And, doubly dying, shall go down
To the vile dust from whence he sprung,
Unwept, unhonored, and unsung.

SIR WALTER SCOTT

THE LAKE ISLE OF INNISFREE

I will arise and go now, and go to Innisfree,
And a small cabin build there, of clay and wattles made;
Nine bean rows will I have there, a hive for the honey bee,
And live alone in the bee-loud glade.

And I shall have some peace there, for peace comes
dropping slow,
Dropping from the veils of the morning to where
the cricket sings;
There midnight's all a-glimmer, and noon a purple glow,
And evening full of the linnet's wings.

I will arise and go now, for always night and day
I hear lake water lapping with low sounds by the shore;
While I stand on the roadway, or on the pavements gray,
I hear it in the deep heart's core.

WILLIAM BUTLER YEATS

HERE IS THE PLACE WHERE LOVELINESS KEEPS HOUSE

Here is the place where Loveliness keeps house,
Between the river and the wooded hills,
Within a valley where the Springtime spills
Her firstling wind-flowers under blossoming boughs;
Where Summer sits braiding her warm, white brows
With bramble-roses; and where Autumn fills
Her lap with asters; and old Winter frills
With crimson haw and hip his snowy blouse.
Here you may meet with Beauty. Here she sits
Gazing upon the moon, or all the day
Tuning a wood-thrush flute, remote, unseen;
Or when the storm is out, 'tis she who flits
From rock to rock, a form of flying spray,
Shouting, beneath the leaves' tumultous green.

MADISON CAWEIN

CHORUS FROM "HIPPOLYTUS"

Could I take me to some cavern for mine hiding,
  In the hill-tops where the Sun scarce hath trod;
Or a cloud make the home of mine abiding,
  As a bird among the bird-droves of God!
    Could I wing me to my rest amid the roar
    Of the deep Adriatic on the shore,
Where the water of Eridanus is clear,
  And Phaethon's sad sisters by his grave
Weep into the river, and each tear
  Gleams, a drop of amber, in the wave.

To the strand of the Daughters of the Sunset,
  The Apple-tree, the singing and the gold;
Where the mariner must stay him from his onset,
  And the red wave is tranquil as of old;
    Yea, beyond that Pillar of the End,
    That Atlas guardeth, would I wend;
Where a voice of living waters never ceaseth
  In God's quiet garden by the sea,
And Earth, the ancient life-giver, increaseth
  Joy among the meadows like a tree.

EURIPIDES
Translation by Gilbert Murray

MY GARDEN

A garden is a lovesome thing, God wot!
  Rose plot,
  Fringed pool,
Fern'd grot—
  The veriest school
  Of peace; and yet the fool
Contends that God is not—
Not God! in gardens! when the eve is cool?
  Nay, but I have a sign;
  'Tis very sure God walks in mine.

THOMAS EDWARD BROWN

AN OLD WOMAN OF THE ROADS

O, to have a little house!
To own the hearth and stool and all!
The heaped up sods upon the fire,
The pile of turf against the wall!

To have a clock with weights and chains
And pendulum swinging up and down!
A dresser filled with shining delph,
Speckled and white and blue and brown!

I could be busy all the day
Clearing and sweeping hearth and floor,
And fixing on their shelf again
My white and blue and speckled store!

I could be quiet there at night
Beside the fire and by myself,
Sure of a bed and loth to leave
The ticking clock and the shining delph!

Och! but I'm weary of mist and dark,
And roads where there's never a house nor bush,
And tired I am of bog and road,
And the crying wind and the lonesome hush!

And I am praying to God on high,
And I am praying Him night and day,
For a little house—a house of my own—
Out of the wind's and the rain's way.

PADRAIC COLUM

PIPPA'S SONG

The year's at the spring,
    And day's at the morn;
Morning's at seven;
    The hill-side's dew-pearled;
The lark's on the wing;
    The snail's on the thorn;
God's in His heaven—
All's right with the world!

ROBERT BROWNING

HOME THOUGHTS, FROM ABROAD

O, to be in England
  Now that April's there,
And whoever wakes in England
  Sees, some morning, unaware,
That the lowest boughs and the brushwood sheaf
  Round the elm tree bole are in tiny leaf,
While the chaffinch sings on the orchard bough
  In England—now!

And after April, when May follows,
  And the whitethroat builds, and all the swallows!
Hark, where my blossom'd pear tree in the hedge
Leans to the field and scatters on the clover
  Blossoms and dewdrops—at the bent spray's edge;
That's the wise thrush; he sings each song twice over,
  Lest you should think he never could recapture
  The first fine careless rapture!

And though the fields look rough with hoary dew,
All will be gay when noontide wakes anew
The buttercups, the little children's dower
—Far brighter than this gaudy melon flower!

ROBERT BROWNING

NEW HORIZONS

When I shall take these hills and make them mine,
So intimately near me, so possessed
That I shall taste the thought of them like wine,
Like holy bread I break within my breast—
Then I shall have no need of coming here
As I have come so many nights, of late,
To strength that stands beyond the hour of fear,
To lonely grandeurs that are kings in state.

For these will be so perfectly my own
That I shall know them near me in the dark:
Their hurts and scars, their strength and rugged stone,
Standing so still and desolate and stark,
That I shall learn what strength and storm are worth,
And how the lonely are the kings of earth.

DAVID MORTON

DAILY BREAD

My little town is homely as another,
But it is old.
And it is full of trees,
And it is covered with sky.
My heart lives in a little house with a
   fire in it,
And a pillow at night,
And is fed daily by laughter and cares,
And the dear needs of children;
But my soul lives out of doors;
Its bread is the beauty of trees,
Its drink, the sky.
There is a moment on winter evenings
When the grey trees on the near hills
   turn rosy,
And all the smoke is blue.
Then I go forth with my basket
   for manna.
And sometimes,
When the air is very clear,
And the moon comes from the dark,
God himself brings me green wine in a
   cup of silver
And holds it for me
While I drink.

KARLE WILSON BAKER

CRADLE-SONG AT TWILIGHT

The child not yet is lulled to rest.
   Too young a nurse, the slender Night
So laxly holds him to her breast
   That throbs with flight.

He plays with her, and will not sleep.
   For other playfellows she sighs;
An unmaternal fondness keep
   Her alien eyes.

ALICE MEYNELL

IF ONCE YOU HAVE SLEPT ON AN ISLAND

If once you have slept on an island
  You'll never be quite the same;
You may look as you looked the day before
  And go by the same old name,

You may bustle about in street and shop;
  You may sit at home and sew,
But you'll see blue water and wheeling gulls
  Wherever your feet may go.

You may chat with the neighbors of this and that
  And close to your fire keep,
But you'll hear ship whistle and lighthouse bell
  And tides beat through your sleep.

Oh, you won't know why, and you can't say how
  Such change upon you came,
But—once you have slept on an island
  You'll never be quite the same!

RACHEL FIELD

ISLANDS

All the islands have run away
  From the land which is their mother;
Out where the lighthouse guards the bay
  They race with one another.

Rocky or wooded, humped and small,
  Edged whitely round with spray,
What should we do if the islands all
  Ran back to land some day?

How would the ships know where to steer?
  Where would the sea-gulls fly?
How flat the sea would look, and queer,
  How lonely under the sky!

RACHEL FIELD

SPRING ECSTASY

Oh, let me run and hide,
  Let me run straight to God;
The weather is so mad with white
  From sky down to the clod!

If but one thing were so,
  Lilac, or thorn out there,
It would not be, indeed,
  So hard to bear.

The weather has gone mad with white;
  The cloud, the highway touch.
White lilac is enough;
  White thorn too much!

                    LIZETTE WOODWORTH REESE

AN APRIL NIGHT

O climb with me, this April night,
The silver ladder of the moon—
All dew and danger and delight:
Above the poplars soon,

Into the lilac-scented sky,
Shall mount her maiden horn,
Frail as a spirit to the eye—
O climb with me till morn!

                    RICHARD LE GALLIENNE

APRIL

Something tapped at my window pane,
  Someone called me without my door,
Someone laughed like the tinkle o'rain,
  The robin echoed it o'er and o'er.

I threw the door and the window wide;
  Sun and the touch of the breeze and then—
"Oh, were you expecting me, dear?" she cried,
  And here was April come back again.

                    THEODOSIA GARRISON

AN APRIL MORNING

Once more in misted April
  The world is growing green,
Along the winding river
  The plumey willows lean.

Beyond the sweeping meadows
  The looming mountains rise,
Like battlements of dreamland
  Against the brooding skies.

In every wooded valley
  The buds are breaking through,
As though the heart of things
  No languor ever knew.

The golden wings and bluebirds
  Call to their heavenly choirs.
The pines are blue and drifted
  With smoke of brushwood fires.

And in my sister's garden
  Where little breezes run,
The golden daffodillies
  Are blowing in the sun.

BLISS CARMAN

Too heartful were the joy of spring,
Did not the cherry blossoms bid us know
How swift and sure must go
Each fairest thing.

If I should come no more,
Plum tree beside my door,
Forget not thou the spring
Faithfully blossoming.

SANETOMO

SPRING
A Color Print—Hiroshige

A yellow raft sails up the bluest stream
  And cherry-blossoms cloud the shore with pink;
The sky grows clearer with a curious gleam,
  The boys come playing to the river brink.

A grayish gull descends to preen and prink,
  Far off, a singing plowman drives his team—
A yellow raft sails up the bluest stream
  And cherry-blossoms cloud the shore with pink . . .

Oh, to be there; far from this tangled scheme
  Of strident days and nights that flare and sink,
Beauty shall lift us with a colored dream;
  And, as we muse, too rapt and wise to think,
A yellow raft sails up the bluest stream
  And cherry-blossoms cloud the shore with pink.

LOUIS UNTERMEYER

A PRAYER AT THE END OF SPRING

If I have been too sombre, Lord,
For daffodils that light the Spring,
If I was all too dull to see
The wiser worship that they bring,
Lord God of laughter and delight,
Remember not this thing.

If I have walked in April ways
Too solemn and too grave, alas,
For all Thy mirthful, careless leaves,
Thy gay and gallant-hearted grass,
Lord, stay me till I learn to heed
They laughter where I pass.

And when there comes another spring
Of tulips rising from the earth,
If I would go too darkly by
To sober things of lesser worth,
Lord, halt me where those pulpits are
To hear Thee preaching mirth.

DAVID MORTON

THE IMMORTAL

Spring has come up from the South again,
  With soft mists in her hair,
And a warm wind in her mouth again
  And budding everywhere.
Spring has come up from the South again
  And her skies are azure fire,
And around her is the awakening
  Of all the world's desire.

Spring has come up from the South again;
  And dreams are in her eyes,
And music is in her mouth again
  Of love, the never-wise.
Spring has come up from the South again
  And bird and flower and bee
Know that she is their life and joy—
  And immortality!

CALE YOUNG RICE

DAYS TOO SHORT

When Primroses are out in Spring
  And small, blue violets come between;
  When merry birds sing on boughs green,
And rills, as soon as born, must sing;

When butterflies will make side-leaps,
  As though escaped from Nature's hand
  Ere perfect quite; and bees will stand
Upon their heads in fragrant deeps;

When small clouds are so silvery white
  Each seems a broken rimmed moon—
  When such things are, this world too soon,
For me, doth wear the veil of Night.

WILLIAM H. DAVIES

SONG OF MAY MORNING

Now the bright morning star, Day's harbinger,
Comes dancing from the East, and leads with her
The flowery May, who from her green lap throws
The yellow cowslip and the pale primrose.
Hail, bounteous May, that doth inspire
Mirth, and youth, and warm desire;
Woods and groves are of thy blessing.
Thus we salute thee with our early song,
And welcome thee, and wish thee long.

JOHN MILTON

And what is so rare as a day in June?
    Then, if ever, come perfect days;
Then Heaven tries earth if it be in tune,
    And over it softly her warm ear lays;
Whether we look or whether we listen,
We hear life murmur, or see it glisten;
Every clod feels a stir of might,
    An instinct within it that reaches and towers,
And, groping blindly above it for light,
    Climbs to a soul in grass and flowers;
The flush of life may well be seen
    Thrilling back over hills and valleys;
The cowslip startles in meadows green,
    The buttercup catches the sun in its chalice,

And there's never a leaf nor a blade too mean
    To be some happy creature's palace;
The little bird sits at his door in the sun,
    Atilt like a blossom among the leaves,
And lets his illumined being o'errun
    With the deluge of summer it receives;
His mate feels the eggs beneath her wings,
And the heart in her dumb breast flutters and sings;
He sings to the wide world, and she to her nest,—
In the nice ear of Nature which song is the best?

From The Vision of Sir Launfal
JAMES RUSSELL LOWELL

SEPTEMBER

The golden-rod is yellow,
  The corn is turning brown,
The trees in apple orchards
  With fruit are bending down.

The gentian's bluest fringes
  Are curling in the sun,
In dusky pods the milkweed
  Its hidden silk has spun.

The sedges flaunt their harvest
  In every meadow-nook,
And asters by the brookside
  Make asters in the brook.

By all these lovely tokens
  September days are here,
With summer's best of weather
  And autumn's best of cheer.

HELEN HUNT JACKSON

AUTUMN MORNING AT CAMBRIDGE

I ran out in the morning, when the air was clean and new
And all the grass was glittering, and grey with autumn dew,
I ran out to the apple tree and pulled an apple down,
And all the bells were ringing in the old grey town.

Down in the town, off the bridges and the grass
They are sweeping up the leaves to let the people pass,
Sweeping up the old leaves, golden-reds and browns,
While the men go to lecture with the wind in their gowns.

FRANCES CORNFORD

"FROST TO-NIGHT"

Apple-green west and an orange bar;
And the crystal eye of a lone, one star . . .
And, "Child, take the shears and cut what you will,
Frost to-night—so clear and dead-still."

Then I sally forth, half said, half proud,
And I come to the velvet, imperial crowd,
The wine-red, the gold, the crimson, the pied,—
The dahlias that reign by the garden-side.

The dahlias I might not touch till to-night!
A gleam of shears in the fading light,
And I gathered them all,—the splendid throng,
And in one great sheaf I bore them along.

. . .
In my garden of Life with its all late flowers
I heed a Voice in the shrinking hours:
"Frost to-night—so clear and dead-still" . . .
Half sad, half proud, my arms I fill.

EDITH M. THOMAS

AUTUMN FIRES

In the other gardens
    And all up the vale,
From the autumn bonfires
    See the smoke trail!

Pleasant summer over
    And all the summer flowers,
The red fire blazes,
    The grey smoke towers.

Sing a song of seasons!
    Something bright in all!
Flowers in the summer,
    Fires in the fall!

ROBERT LOUIS STEVENSON

AUTUMN

Then came the Autumn all in yellow clad,
As though he joyed in his plenteous store,
Laden with fruits that made him laugh, full glad
That he had banished hunger, which to-fore
Had by the belly oft him pinched sore:
Upon his head a wreath, that was enroll'd
With ears of corn of every sort, he bore;
And in his hand a sickle he did hold,
To reap the ripen'd fruits the which the earth
　had yold.

EDMUND SPENSER

MAPLE LEAVES

October turned my maple's leaves to gold;
The most are gone now; here and there one lingers:
Soon these will slip from out the twigs' weak hold,
Like coins between a dying miser's fingers.

THOMAS BAILEY ALDRICH

A PRAYER FOR NOVEMBER

While still there is a fire upon my hearth
Where friends may warm themselves when raw winds
　bite and blow,
While still my hands and mind have strength enough
To earn the loaf of bread that I will share,
While still my heart is free from bitterness and hate
For suffering and pain I have endured,
While still I love the autumn woods and windy days
As well as all the soothing promises of spring,
Then can I still be glad,
And thank Thee, Lord.

ROWE WRIGHT

WINDFALLS

The day we picked up windfalls
We took a lunch along,
We heard the whirr of pheasants' wings
Melodious as a song;

And all day under frosty skies
We filled our sacks with gleanings
Of McIntosh and Scarlet Kings
And Northern Spies and Greenings;

Red-streaked Cayugas, Jonathans,
And Flowers of Genesee,
Till we had combed the grass beneath
Each overflowing tree.

And then the dusk had fallen
And we crept into our beds,
And all the lovely apple names
Went singing through our heads.

ELISABETH G. PALMER

THE HARVEST

Oh, 'tis sweet, when fields are ringing
With merry cricket's singing,
Oft to mark with curious eye
If the vine-tree's time be nigh:
Here is now the fruit whose birth
Cost a pang to Mother Earth.

Sweet it is, too, to be telling,
How the luscious figs are swelling;
Then to riot without measure
In the rich, nectareous treasure,
While our grateful voices chime,—
Happy season! blessed time.

ARISTOPHANES

OCTOBER'S BRIGHT BLUE WEATHER

O suns and skies and clouds of June,
  And flowers of June together,
Ye cannot rival for one hour
  October's bright blue weather;

When loud the bumblebee makes haste,
  Belated, thriftless, vagrant,
And goldenrod is dying fast,
  And lanes with grapes are fragrant;

When gentians roll their fringes tight,
  To save them for the morning,
And chestnuts fall from satin burrs
  Without a sound of warning;

When on the ground red apples lie
  In piles like jewels shining;
And redder still on old stone walls
  Are leaves of woodbine twining;

When all the lovely wayside things
  Their white-winged seeds are sowing,
And in the fields, still green and fair,
  Late aftermaths are growing;

When springs run low, and on the brooks,
  In idle golden freighting,
Bright leaves sink noiseless in the hush
  Of woods, for winter waiting;

When comrades seek sweet country haunts,
  By twos and twos together,
And count like misers, hour by hour,
  October's bright blue weather;

O sun and skies and flowers of June,
  Count all your boasts together,
Love loveth best of all the year
  October's bright blue weather.

HELEN HUNT JACKSON

DOWN TO SLEEP

November woods are bare and still,
  November days are clear and bright,
Each noon burns up the morning's chill,
  The morning's snow is gone by night,
  Each day my steps grow slow, grow light,
  As through the woods I reverent creep,
  Watching all things "lie down to sleep."

I never knew before what beds,
  Fragrant to smell and soft to touch,
The forest sifts and shapes and spreads.
  I never knew before, how much
  Of human sound there is, in such
Low tones as through the forest sweep,
  When all wild things "lie down to sleep."

Each day I find new coverlids
  Tucked in, and more sweet eyes shut tight.
Sometimes the viewless mother bids
  Her ferns kneel down full in my sight,
  I hear their chorus of "good night,"
  And half I smile and half I weep,
  Listening while they "lie down to sleep."

November woods are bare and still,
  November days are bright and good,
Life's noon burns up life's morning chill,
  Life's night rests feet that long have stood,
  Some warm, soft bed in field or wood
  The mother will not fail to keep
  Where we can "lay us down to sleep."

HELEN HUNT JACKSON

THE SNOWSTORM

Announced by all the trumpets of the sky,
Arrives the snow, and driving o'er the fields,
Seems nowhere to alight; the whited air
Hides hills and woods, the river and the heaven,
And veils the farmhouse at the garden's end.
The sled and traveler stopped, the courier's feet
Delayed, all friends shut out, the housemates sit
Around the radiant fireplace, inclosed
In a tumultous privacy of storm.

RALPH WALDO EMERSON

STOPPING BY WOODS ON A SNOWY EVENING

Whose woods these are I think I know.
His house is in the village though;
He will not see me stopping here
To watch his woods fill up with snow.

My little horse must think it queer
To stop without a farmhouse near
Between the woods and frozen lake
The darkest evening of the year.

He gives his harness bells a shake
To ask if there is some mistake.
The only other sound's the sweep
Of easy wind and downy flake.

The woods are lovely, dark and deep,
But I have promises to keep.
And miles to go before I sleep,
And miles to go before I sleep.

ROBERT FROST

THE WINTER FIRE

A fire's a good companionable friend,
A comfortable friend, who meets your face
With welcome glad, and makes the poorest shed
As pleasant as a palace! Are you cold?
He warms you—Weary? he refreshes you,
Are you in darkness? he gives light to you—
In a strange land? he wears a face that is
Familiar from your childhood. Are you poor?—
What matters it to him? He knows no difference
Between an emperor and the poorest beggar!
Where is the friend, that bears the name of man,
Will do as much for you?

MARY HOWITT

HILLS

I never loved your plains!—
  Your gentle valleys,
Your drowsy country lanes
  And pleached alleys.

I want my hills!—the trail
  That scorns the hollow.
Up, up the ragged shale
  Where few will follow.

Up, over wooded crest
  And mossy boulder
With strong thigh, heaving chest,
  And swinging shoulder.

So let me hold my way,
  By nothing halted,
Until, at close of day,
  I stand, exalted.

High on my hills of dream—
  Dear hills that know me!
And then, how fair will seem
  The lands below me.

How pure at vesper time,
  The far bells chiming!
God give me hills to climb
  And strength for climbing!

ARTHUR GUITERMAN

The Navaho say:

In beauty (happily) I walk.
With beauty before me I walk.
With beauty behind me I walk.
With beauty below me I walk.
With beauty above me I walk.
It is finished (again) in beauty.
It is finished in beauty.

UNKNOWN

AFTER SUNSET

I have an understanding with the hills
At evening, when the slanted radiance fills
Their hollows, and the great winds let them be,
And they are quiet and look down at me.
Oh, when I see the patience in their eyes
Out of the centuries that made them wise,
They lend me hoarded memory, and I learn
Their thoughts of granite and their whims of fern,
And why a dream of forests must endure
Though every tree be slain; and how the pure,
Invisible beauty has a word so brief,
A flower can say it, or a shaken leaf,
But few may ever snare it in a song,
Though for the quest a life is not too long.
When the blue hills grow tender, when they pull
The twilight close with gesture beautiful,
And shadows are their garments, and the air
Deepens, and the wild veery is at prayer,
Their arms are strong around me; and I know
That somehow I shall follow when they go
To the still land beyond the evening star,
Where everlasting hills and valleys are,
And silence may not hurt us any more,
And terror shall be past, and grief and war.

GRACE HAZARD CONKLING

HILL HUNGER

I want to stride the hills! My feet cry out
   For hills! Oh, I am sick to death of streets:
The nausea of pavements and people always about;
   The savagery of mortar and steel that beats
Me under, hedges me in; the iron shiver
   Of traffic!—I want to stride the hills, I want
Hills toned frantic silver or a quiver
   Of scarlet; hills that hunger and grow gaunt!
I am tired of steps and steps, and a thousand flights
   Of stairs resounding, shuffling, quarreling
With shoes. I want a hill on windy nights,
   When April pauses with me, clamoring
Over the purple side of the top, until
   We pull ourselves up by a star—the hill! the hill!

JOSEPH AUSLANDER

THE MOUNTAINS ARE A LONELY FOLK

The mountains they are silent folk,
  They stand afar—alone;
And the clouds that kiss their brows at night
  Hear neither sigh nor groan.
Each bears him in his ordered place
  As soldiers do, and bold and high
They fold their forests round their feet
  And bolster up the sky.

ROBERT FROST

THE FOREST

We are the hosts innumerable who ride
Upon the hills—who stride
The plains and surge upon the mountainside;
We are the onward-sweeping tide
Of ceaseless growth, the countless entities
Of all the rolling, emerald seas
Of timberland—we are the Trees!

ANTHONY EUWER

GOOD COMPANY

Today I have grown taller from walking with the trees,
  The seven sister-poplars who go softly in a line;
And I think my heart is whiter for its parley with a star
  That trembled out at nightfall and hung above the pine.

The call-note of a red-bird from the cedars in the dusk
  Woke his happy mate within me to an answer free and fine;
And a sudden angel beckoned from a column of blue smoke—
  Lord, who am I that they should stoop—these holy folk
  of Thine?

KARLE WILSON BAKER

IN THE WOODLAND

In the forest bower I see
  Little ring plots fenced around
So that shrub and sapling tree
  Thrive in safe and happy ground.

And I wonder, cannot I,
  Keep some little space apart
Open to the wind and sky
  For the growing of my heart?

AUTHOR UNKNOWN

MOUNTAIN AIR

Tell me of Progress if you will
But give me sunshine on a hill—
The grey rocks spiring to the blue,
The scent of larches, pinks, and dew,
And summer sighing in the trees,
And snowy breath on every breeze.

Take towns, and all that you'll find there,
And leave me sun and mountain air!

JOHN GALSWORTHY

THE CEDARS

All down the years the fragrance came,
The mingled fragrance, with a flame,
Of Cedars breathing in the sun,
The Cedar-trees of Lebanon.

O thirst of song in bitter air,
And hope, wing-hurt from iron care,
What balm of myrrh and honey, won
From far-off trees of Lebanon!

Not from these eyelids yet have I
Ever beheld that early sky.
Why do they call me through the sun?—
Even the trees of Lebanon?

JOSEPHINE PRESTON PEABODY

LEAVES

One by one, like leaves from a tree,
All my faiths have forsaken me;
But the stars above my head
Burn in white and delicate red,
And beneath my feet the earth
Brings the sturdy grass to birth.
I who was content to be
But a silken-singing tree,
But a rustle of delight
In the wistful heart of night,
I have lost the leaves that knew
Touch of rain and weight of dew.
Blinded by a leafy crown
I looked neither up nor down—
But the leaves that fall and die
Have left me room to see the sky!
Now for the first time I know
Stars above and earth below.

SARA TEASDALE

A BALLAD OF TREES AND THE MASTER

Into the woods my Master went,
Clean forspent, forspent,
Into the woods my Master came,
Forspent with love and shame.
But the olives they were not blind to Him;
The little grey leaves were kind to Him;
The thorn-tree had a mind to Him
When into the woods He came.

Out of the woods my Master went,
And He was well content.
Out of the woods my Master came,
Content with death and shame.
When Death and Shame would woo Him last,
From under the trees they drew Him last:
'Twas on a tree they slew Him—last
When out of the woods He came.

SIDNEY LANIER

THE PLANTING OF THE APPLE-TREE

Come, let us plant the apple-tree.
Cleave the tough greensward with the spade;
Wide let its hollow bed be made;
There gently lay the roots, and there
Sift the dark mould with kindly care,
    And press it o'er them tenderly,
As, round the sleeping infant's feet,
We softly fold the cradle-sheet;
    So plant we the apple-tree.

What plant we in this apple-tree?
Buds, which the breath of summer days
Shall lengthen into leafy sprays;
Boughs where the thrush, with crimson breast,
Shall haunt, and sing, and hide her nest;
    We plant, upon the sunny lea,
A shadow for the noontide hour,
A shelter from the summer shower,
    When we plant the apple-tree.

• • •

What plant we in this apple-tree?
Fruits that shall swell in sunny June,
And redden in the August noon,
And drop, when gentle airs come by,
That fan the blue September sky,
    While children come, with cries of glee,
And seek them where the fragrant grass
Betrays their bed to those who pass,
    At the foot of the apple-tree.

And when, above this apple-tree,
The winter stars are quivering bright,
And winds go howling through the night,
Girls, whose young eyes o'erflow with mirth,
Shall peel its fruit by cottage-hearth,
    And guests in prouder homes shall see,
Heaped with the grape of Cintra's vine
And golden orange of the line,
    The fruit of the apple-tree.

WILLIAM CULLEN BRYANT

THE TREE

I love thee when thy swelling buds appear,
And one by one their tender leaves unfold,
As if they knew that warmer suns were near,
Nor longer sought to hide from winter's cold;
And when with darker growth thy leaves are seen
To veil from view the early robin's nest,
I love to lie beneath thy waving screen,
With limbs by summer's heat and toil oppressed;
And when the autumn winds have stripped thee bare,
And round thee lies the smooth, untrodden snow,
When nought is thine that made thee once so fair,
I love to watch thy shadowy form below,
And through thy leafless arms to look above
On stars that brighter beam when most we need their
        love.

JONES VERY

WHAT DO WE PLANT?

What do we plant, when we plant the tree?
We plant the ship, which will cross the sea.
We plant the mast to carry the sails;
We plant the planks to withstand the gales—
The keel, the keelson, the beam, the knee;
We plant the ship when we plant the tree.

What do we plant when we plant the tree?
We plant the houses for you and me.
We plant the rafters, the shingles, the floors,
We plant the studding, the lath, the doors,
The beams and siding, all parts that be;
We plant the house when we plant the tree.

What do we plant when we plant the tree?
A thousand things that we daily see;
We plant the spire that out-towers the crag,
We plant the staff for our country's flag.
We plant the shade, from the hot sun free;
We plant all these when we plant the tree.

HENRY ABBEY

AN APPLE ORCHARD IN THE SPRING

Have you seen an apple orchard in the spring?
                                    In the spring?
An English apple orchard in the spring?
   When the spreading trees are hoary
   With their wealth of promising glory,
And the mavis sings its story,
                                    In the spring.

Have you plucked the apple blossoms in the spring?
                                    In the spring?
And caught their subtle odours in the spring?
   Pink buds pouting at the light,
   Crumpled petals baby white,
   Just to touch them a delight—
                                    In the spring.

Have you walked beneath the blossoms in the spring?
                                    In the spring?
Beneath the apple blossoms in the spring?
   When the pink cascades are falling,
   And the silver brooklets brawling,
   And the cuckoo bird soft calling,
                                    In the spring.

If you have not, then you know not, in the spring,
                                    In the spring,
Half the colour, beauty, wonder of the spring,
   No sweet sight can I remember
   Half so precious, half so tender,
   As the apple blossoms render
                                    In the spring.
                                    WILLIAM MARTIN

The poplars shiver and turn their leaves,
And the wind through the belfry moans and grieves.
The gray dust whirls in the market square,
And the silver hearts are covered with care
By thick tarpaulins. Once again
The bay is black under heavy rain.
                                    JAMES RUSSELL LOWELL

WHOLE DUTY OF BERKSHIRE BROOKS

To build the trout a crystal stair;
To comb the hillside's thick green hair;
To water jewel-weed and rushes;
To teach first notes to baby thrushes;
To flavor raspberry and apple
And make a whirling pool to dapple
With scattered gold of late October;
To urge wise laughter on the sober
And lend a dream to those who laugh;
To chant the beetle's epitaph;
To mirror the blue dragonfly,
Frail air-plane of a slender sky;
Over the stones to lull and leap
Herding the bubbles like white sheep;
The claims of worry to deny,
And whisper sorrow into sleep!

GRACE HAZARD CONKLING

THE BROOK

I come from haunts of coot and hern;
    I make a sudden sally,
And sparkle out among the fern
    To bicker down a valley.

By thirty hills I hurry down,
    Or slip between the ridges;
By twenty thorps, a little town,
    And half a hundred bridges.

Till last by Philip's farm I flow
    To join the brimming river;
For men may come, and men may go,
    But I go on forever.

I chatter over stony ways,
    In little sharps and trebles;
I bubble into eddying bays;
    I babble on the pebbles.

With many a curve my bank I fret
  By many a field and fallow,
And many a fairy foreland set
  With willow-weed and mallow.

I chatter, chatter, as I flow
  To join the brimming river;
For men may come, and men may go,
  But I go on forever.

I wind about, and in and out,
  With here a blossom sailing,
And here and there a lusty trout,
  And here and there a grayling.

And here and there a foamy flake
  Upon me as I travel,
With many a silvery water-break
  Above the golden gravel.

And draw them all along, and flow
  To join the brimming river;
For men may come, and men may go,
  But I go on forever.

I steal by lawns and grassy plots,
  I slide by hazel covers,
I move the sweet forget-me-nots
  That grow for happy lovers.

I slip, I slide, I gloom, I glance,
  Among my skimming swallows;
I make the netted sunbeams dance
  Against my sandy shallows.

I murmur under moon and stars
  In brambly wildernesses;
I linger by my shingly bars,
  I loiter round my cresses;

And out again I curve and flow
  To join the brimming river,
For men may come, and men may go,
  But I go on forever.

ALFRED TENNYSON

WHERE GO THE BOATS?

Dark brown is the river,
  Golden is the sand.
It flows along forever,
  With trees on either hand.

Green leaves a-floating,
  Castles of the foam,
Boats of mine a-boating—
  When will all come home?

On goes the river,
  And out past the mill,
Away down the valley,
  Away down the hill.

Away down the river,
  A hundred miles or more,
Other little children
  Shall bring my boats ashore.

ROBERT LOUIS STEVENSON

Could I but return to my woods once more,
And dwell in their depths as I have dwelt,
Kneel in their mosses as I have knelt,
Sit where the cool white rivers run,
Away from the world and half hid from the sun,
Hear winds in the wood of my storm-torn shore,
To tread where only the red man trod,
To say no word, but listen to God!
Glad to the heart with listening—
It seems to me that I then could sing,
And sing as never man sung before.

JOAQUIN MILLER

THE SANDPIPER

Across the lonely beach we flit,
 One little sandpiper and I,
And fast I gather, bit by bit,
 The scattered drift-wood bleached and dry.
The wild waves reach their hands for it,
 The wild wind raves, the tide runs high,
As up and down the beach we flit,
 One little sandpiper and I.

Above our heads the sullen clouds
 Scud, black and swift, across the sky;
Like silent ghosts in misty shrouds
 Stand out the white light-houses high.
Almost as far as eye can reach
 I see the close-reefed vessels fly,
As fast we flit across the beach,
 One little sandpiper and I.

I watch him as he skims along,
 Uttering his sweet and mournful cry;
He starts not at my fitful song,
 Nor flash of fluttering drapery.
He has no thought of any wrong,
 He scans me with a fearless eye;
Staunch friends are we, well tried and strong,
 The little sandpiper and I.

Comrade, where wilt thou be tonight,
 When the loosed storm breaks furiously?
My drift-wood fire will burn so bright!
 To what warm shelter canst thou fly?
I do not fear for thee, though wroth
 The tempest rushes through the sky;
For are we not God's children both,
 Thou, little sandpiper, and I?

CELIA THAXTER

THE DONKEY

When fishes flew and forests walked
And figs grew upon thorn,
Some moment when the moon was blood
Then surely I was born;

With monstrous head and sickening cry
And ears like errant wings,
The devil's walking parody
On all four-footed things.

The tattered outlaw of the earth,
Of ancient crooked will;
Starve, scourge, deride me: I am dumb,
I keep my secret still.

Fools! For I also had my hour;
One far fierce hour and sweet:
There was a shout about my ears,
And palms before my feet.

GILBERT KEITH CHESTERTON

WILD GEESE

How oft against the sunset sky or moon
    I watched the moving zigzag of spread wings
In unforgotten Autumns gone too soon,
    In unforgotten Springs!
Creatures of desolation, far they fly
    Above all lands bound by the curling foam;
In misty fens, wild moors and trackless sky
    These wild things have their home.
They know the tundra of Siberian coasts,
    And tropic marshes by the Indian seas;
They know the clouds and night and starry hosts
    From Crux to Pleiades.
Dark flying rune against the western glow—
    It tells the sweep and loneliness of things,
Symbol of Autumns vanished long ago.
    Symbol of coming Springs!

FREDERICK PETERSON

A BLACKBIRD SUDDENLY

Heaven is in my hand, and I
Touched a heart-beat of the sky,
Hearing a blackbird cry.

Strange, beautiful, unquiet thing,
Lone flute of God, how can you sing
Winter to Spring?

You have outdistanced every voice and word,
And given my spirit wings until it stirred
Like you—a bird.

JOSEPH AUSLANDER

FROM "EARTH"

Grasshopper, your fairy song
And my poem alike belong
To the deep and silent earth
From which all poetry has birth;
All we say and all we sing
Is but as the murmuring
Of that drowsy heart of hers
When from her deep dreams she stirs;
If we sorrow, or rejoice,
You and I are but her voice.

JOHN HALL WHEELOCK

LITTLE THINGS

Little things that run and quail
And die in silence and despair;
Little things that fight and fail
And fall on sea and earth and air:
All trapped and frightened little things,
The mouse, the coney, hear our prayer:
As we forgive those done to us,
The lamb, the linnet, and the hare,
Forgive us all our trespasses,
Little creatures everywhere.

JAMES STEPHENS

THE EAGLE

He clasps the crag with crooked hands;
Close to the sun in lonely lands,
Ringed with the azure world, he stands.

The wrinkled sea beneath him crawls;
He watches from his mountain walls,
And like a thunderbolt he falls.

ALFRED TENNYSON

A VISIT FROM THE SEA

Far from the loud sea beaches
    Where he goes fishing and crying,
Here in the inland garden
    Why is the sea-gull flying?

Here are no fish to dive for;
    Here is the corn and lea;
Here are the green trees rustling.
    Hie away home to sea!

Fresh is the river water
    And quiet among the rushes;
This is no home for the sea-gull
    But for the rooks and thrushes.

Pity the bird that has wandered!
    Pity the sailor ashore!
Hurry him home to the ocean,
    Let him come here no more!

High on the sea-cliff ledges
    The white gulls are trooping and crying,
Here among rooks and roses,
    Why is the sea-gull flying?

ROBERT LOUIS STEVENSON

THE HOUSEKEEPER

The frugal snail, with forecast of repose,
Carries his house with him where'er he goes;
Peeps out,—and if there comes a shower of rain,
Retreats to his small domicile amain.
Touch but a tip of him, a horn,—'tis well,—
He curls up in his sanctuary shell.
He's his own landlord, his own tenant; stay
Long as he will he dreads no Quarter Day.
Himself he boards and lodges; both invites
And feasts himself; sleeps with himself o'nights.
He spares the upholsterer trouble to procure
Chattels; himself is his own furniture,
And his sole riches. Whereso'er he roam,—
Knock when you will,—he's sure to be at home.

CHARLES LAMB

DAISIES

Over the shoulders and slopes of the dune
I saw the white daisies go down to the sea,
A host in the sunshine, an army in June,
The people God sends us to set our hearts free.

The bobolinks rallied them up from the dell,
The orioles whistled them out of the wood;
And all of their singing was, "Earth, it is well!"
And all of their dancing was, "Life, thou art good!"

BLISS CARMAN

PEACH BLOSSOM AFTER RAIN

Peach blossom after rain
  Is deeper red;
The willow fresher green;
  Twittering overhead;
And fallen petals lie wind-blown,
Unswept upon the courtyard stone.

Chinese Lyrics translated by
HELEN WADDELL

DAFFODILS

I wander'd lonely as a cloud
    That floats on high o'er vales and hills,
When all at once I saw a crowd,
    A host, of golden daffodils,
Beside the lake, beneath the trees,
Fluttering and dancing in the breeze.

Continuous as the stars that shine
    And twinkle on the milky way,
They stretch'd in never ending line
    Along the margin of a bay:
Ten thousand saw I at a glance,
Tossing their heads in sprightly dance.

The waves beside them danced, but they
    Outdid the sparkling waves in glee;
A poet could not but be gay
    In such a jocund company.
I gazed—and gazed,—but little thought
What wealth the show to me had brought.

For oft, when on my couch I lie
    In vacant or in pensive mood,
They flash upon that inward eye
    Which is the bliss of solitude;
And then my heart with pleasure fills
And dances with the daffodils.

WILLIAM WORDSWORTH

FLOWER IN THE CRANNIED WALL

Flower in the crannied wall,
I pluck you out of the crannies;
Hold you here, root and all, in my hand,
Little flower—but if I could understand
What you are, root and all, and all in all,
I should know what God and man is.

ALFRED TENNYSON

A FLOWER IS LOOKING THROUGH THE GROUND

A flower is looking through the ground,
Blinking at the April weather;
Now a child has seen the flower:
Now they go and play together.

Now it seems the flower will speak,
And will call the child its brother—
But, oh strange forgetfulness!—
They don't recognize each other.

HAROLD MONRO

ALDERBARAN AT DUSK

Thou art the star for which all evening waits—
    A star of peace, come tenderly and soon,
    Nor heed the drowsy and enchanted moon,
Who dreams in silver at the eastern gates
Ere yet she brim with light the blue estates
    Abandoned by the eagles of the noon.

But shine thou swiftly on the darkling dune
And woodlands where the twilight hesitates.

Above the wide and ruby lake to-West,
    Wherein the sunset waits reluctantly,
        Stir silently the purple wings of Night.
She stands afar, upholding to her breast,
    As mighty murmurs reach her from the sea,
        Thy lone and everlasting rose of light.

GEORGE STERLING

DUSK

A pitchy pine branch laid against
The rich red orange of an autumn moon;
The wild ducks call across the marsh,
And from the purple shadows of the wood
Three spotted deer mince to the water's edge.

COBALLERO

A DAISY'S SONG
(A Fragment)

The sun, with his great eye,
Sees not so much as I;
And the moon, all silver-proud
Might as well be in a cloud.

And O the spring—the spring!
I lead the life of a king!
Couch'd in the teeming grass,
I spy each pretty lass.

I look where no one dares,
And I stare where no one stares,
And when the night is nigh
Lambs bleat my lullaby.

JOHN KEATS

MY BED IS A BOAT

My bed is like a little boat;
  Nurse helps me in when I embark;
She girds me in my sailor's coat
  And starts me in the dark.

At night, I go abroad and say
  Good night to all my friends on shore;
I shut my eyes and sail away
  And see and hear no more.

And sometimes things to bed I take,
  As prudent sailors have to do;
Perhaps a slice of wedding-cake,
  Perhaps a toy or two.

All night across the dark we steer;
  But when the day returns at last,
Safe in my room, beside the pier,
  I find my vessel fast.

ROBERT LOUIS STEVENSON

THE FIRST DANDELION

Simple and fresh and fair from winter's close emerging,
As if no artifice of fashion, business, politics, had ever been,
Forth from its sunny nook of shelter'd grass—innocent,
    golden, calm as the dawn,
The spring's first dandelion shows its trustful face.

WALT WHITMAN

The stars are forth, the moon above the tops
Of the snow-shining mountains—Beautiful!
I linger yet with Nature, for the night
Hath been to me a more familiar face
Than that of man: and in her starry shade
Of dim and solitary loveliness,
I learned the language of another world.

LORD BYRON

Teach me your mood, O patient stars,
    Who climb each night the ancient sky,
Leaving on space no shade, no scars,
    No trace of age, no fear to die.

RALPH WALDO EMERSON

The wonder of an ancient awe
    Takes hold upon him when he sees
In the cold autumn dusk arise
    Orion and the Pleiades;

Or when along the southern rim
    Of the mysterious summer night
He marks, above the sleeping world,
    Antares with his scarlet light.

BLISS CARMAN

DAISIES

At evening when I go to bed
I see the stars shine overhead;
They are the little daisies white
That dot the meadow of the Night.

And often while I'm dreaming so,
Across the sky the Moon will go;
It is a lady, sweet and fair,
Who comes to gather daisies there.

For, when at morning I arise,
There's not a star left in the skies;
She's picked them all and dropped them down
Into the meadows of the town.

FRANK DEMPSTER SHERMAN

NIGHT MAGIC

The apples falling from the tree
   Make such a heavy bump at night
I always am surprised to see
   They are so little, when it's light.

And all the dark just sings and sings
   So loud, I can not see at all
How frogs and crickets and such things
   That make the noise can be so small.

Then my own room looks larger, too—
   Corners so dark and far away—
I wonder if things really do
   Grow up at night and shrink by day.

For I dream sometimes, just as clear,
   I'm bigger than the biggest men—
Then mother says, "Wake up, my dear!"
   And I'm a little boy again.

AMELIA JOSEPHINE BURR

THE NIGHT WILL NEVER STAY

The night will never stay,
  The night will still go by,
Though with a million stars
  You pin it to the sky,
Though you bind it with the blowing wind
  And buckle it with the moon,
The night will slip away
  Like sorrow or a tune.

ELEANOR FARJEON

A NET TO SNARE THE MOONLIGHT

  (What the man of faith said)
The dew, the rain and moonlight
All prove our Father's mind.
The dew, the rain and moonlight
Descend to bless mankind.

  Come, let us see that all men
  Have land to catch the rain,
  Have grass to snare the spheres of dew,
  And fields spread for the grain.

  Yea, we would give to each poor man
  Ripe wheat and poppies red, —
  A peaceful place at evening
  With stars just overhead:

  A net to snare the moonlight,
  A sod spread to the sun,
  A place of toil by daytime,
  Of dreams when toil is done.

VACHEL LINDSAY

DAYBREAK

Day had awakened all things that be,
The lark, and the thrush, and the swallow free,
And the milkmaid's song, and the mower's scythe,
And the matin bell and the mountain bee:
Fireflies were quenched on the dewy corn,
Glowworms went out, on the river's brim.
Like lamps which a student forgets to trim:
The beetle forgot to wind his horn,
The crickets were still in the meadow and hill:
Like a flock of rooks at a farmer's gun,
Night's dreams and terrors, every one,
Fled from the brains which are its prey,
From the lamp's death to the morning ray.

PERCY BYSSHE SHELLEY

NIGHT

How beautiful is night!
A dewy freshness fills the silent air;
No mist obscures, nor cloud, nor speck, nor stain,
Breaks the serene of heaven:
In full-orb'd glory yonder Moon divine
Rolls through the dark-blue depths.
Beneath her steady ray
The desert-circle spreads,
Like the round ocean, girdled with the sky.
How beautiful is night!

ROBERT SOUTHEY

FOG

The fog comes
on little cat feet.

It sits looking
over harbor and city
on silent haunches
and then moves on.

CARL SANDBURG

MONOTONE

The monotone of the rain is beautiful,
And the sudden rise and slow relapse
Of the long multitudinous rain.

The sun on the hills is beautiful,
Or a captured sunset, sea-flung,
Bannered with fire and gold.

A face I know is beautiful—
With fire and gold of sky and sea,
And the peace of long warm rain.

CARL SANDBURG

GREY GIRL

A little Grey Girl in a little Grey Cloak
Came over the hill by the lane—
She carried a bundle which suddenly broke.
"Oh dear," cried the Girl in the little Grey Cloak,
"I am losing my beautiful rain!"

FLORENCE HOATSON

RAIN

The rain is raining all around,
It falls on field and tree,
It rains on the umbrellas here,
And on the ships at sea.

ROBERT LOUIS STEVENSON

WHO LOVES THE RAIN

Who loves the rain,
And loves his home,
And looks on life with quiet eyes,
Him will I follow through the storm;
And at his hearth-fire keep me warm;
Nor hell nor heaven shall that soul surprise,
Who loves the rain,
And loves his home,
And looks on life with quiet eyes.

FRANCES SHAW

RAIN IN THE NIGHT

Raining, raining,
All night long;
Sometimes loud, sometimes soft,
Just like a song.

There'll be rivers in the gutters
And lakes along the street,
It will make our lazy kitty
Wash his little dirty feet.

The roses will wear diamonds
Like kings and queens at court;
But the pansies all get muddy
Because they are so short.

I'll sail my boat tomorrow
In wonderful new places,
But first I'll take my watering-pot
And wash the pansies' faces.

AMELIA JOSEPHINE BURR

SILVER

Slowly, silently, now the moon
Walks the night in her silver shoon;
This way, and that, she peers and sees
Silver fruit upon silver trees;
One by one the casements catch
Her beams beneath the silvery thatch;
Couched in his kennel, like a log,
With paws of silver sleeps the dog;
From their shadowy cote the white breasts peep
Of doves in a silver-feathered sleep;
A harvest mouse goes scampering by,
With silver claws, and a silver eye;
And moveless fish in the water gleam,
By silver reeds in a silver stream.

WALTER DE LA MARE

WIND

Wind, wind—heather gypsy
   Whistling in my tree!
All the heart of me is tipsy
   On the sound of thee.
Sweet with the scent of clover,
   Salt with the breath of sea,
Wind, wind—wayman lover,
   Whistling in my tree!

JOHN GALSWORTHY

THE WIND

I saw you toss the kites on high
And blow the birds about the sky;
And all around I heard you pass,
Like ladies' skirts across the grass—
   O wind, a-blowing all day long,
   O wind, that sings so loud a song!

I saw the different things you did,
But always you yourself you hid.
I felt you push, I heard you call,
I could not see yourself at all—
   O wind, a-blowing all day long,
   O wind, that sings so loud a song!

O you that are so strong and cold,
O blower, are you young or old?
Are you a beast of field and tree,
Or just a stronger child than me?
   O wind, a-blowing all day long,
   O wind, that sings so loud a song!

ROBERT LOUIS STEVENSON

I love and understand
One joy: with staff and scrip
To walk a wild west land,
The winds my fellowship.

LIONEL JOHNSON

THE WIND

Who has seen the wind?
  Neither I nor you:
But when the leaves hang trembling,
  The wind is passing through.

Who has seen the wind?
  Neither you nor I:
But when the trees bow down their heads,
  The wind is passing by.

CHRISTINA G. ROSSETTI

BEFORE THE RAIN

We knew it would rain, for all the morn,
  A spirit on slender ropes of mist
Was lowering its golden buckets down
  Into the vapory amethyst

Of marshes and swamps and dismal fens—
  Scooping the dew that lay in the flowers,
Dipping the jewels out of the sea,
  To sprinkle them over the land in showers.

We knew it would rain, for the poplars showed
  The white of their leaves, the amber grain
Shrunk in the wind—and the lightning now
  Is tangled in tremulous skeins of rain!

THOMAS BAILEY ALDRICH

The spring rain
Which hangs to the branches
Of the green willow
Looks like pearls
Threaded on a string.

LADY ISE—C 1000 A.D.

OH, GRAY AND TENDER IS THE RAIN

Oh, gray and tender is the rain,
That drips, drips on the pane!
A hundred things come in the door,
The scent of herbs, the thought of yore.

I see the pool out in the grass,
A bit of broken glass;
The red flags running wet and straight,
Down to the little flapping gate.

Lombardy poplars tall and three,
Across the road I see;
There is no loveliness so plain
As a tall poplar in the rain.

But Oh, the hundred things and more,
That come in at the door!—
The smack of mint, old joy, old pain,
Caught in the gray and tender rain.

LIZETTE WOODWORTH REESE

A SUDDEN SHOWER

Barefooted boys scud up the street
    Or scurry under sheltering sheds;
And school-girl faces, pale and sweet,
    Gleam from the shawls about their heads.

Doors bang; and mother-voices call
    From alien homes; and rusty gates
Are slammed; and high above it all,
    The thunder grim reverberates.

And then, abrupt,—the rain! the rain!—
    The earth lies gasping; and the eyes
Behind the steaming window-pane
    Smile at the trouble of the skies.

The highway smokes; sharp echoes ring;
    The cattle bawl and cow-bells clank;
And into town comes galloping
    The farmer's horse, with steaming flank.

The swallow dips beneath the eaves
    And flirts his plumes and folds his wings;
And under the Catawba leaves
    The caterpillar curls and clings.

The bumblebee is pelted down
    The wet stem of the hollyhock;
And sullenly, in spattered brown,
    The cricket leaps the garden-walk.

Within, the baby claps his hands
    And crows with rapture strange and vague;
Without, beneath the rose-bush stands
    A dripping rooster on one leg.

JAMES WHITCOMB RILEY

A CHRISTMAS FOLK-SONG

The Little Jesus came to town;
The wind blew up, the wind blew down;
Out in the street the wind was bold;
Now who would house Him from the cold?

Then opened wide a stable door,
Fair were the rushes on the floor;
The Ox put forth a horned head;
"Come, Little Lord, here make Thy bed."

Up rose the Sheep were folded near;
"Thou Lamb of God, come, enter here."
He entered there to rush and reed,
Who was the Lamb of God indeed.

The Little Jesus came to town;
With ox and sheep He laid Him down;
Peace to the byre, peace to the fold,
For that they housed Him from the cold!

LIZETTE WOODWORTH REESE

TWELFTH NIGHT

Three wild kings came to the town,
Riding with one mind;
Scarlet, cinnamon, stormy blue,
Stream their cloaks behind.

Call the wild kings through the night,
Standing each at door;
"Open. There is here a gift,
Kept for you of yore."

"Here is gold," saith the wild king,
He the blue-clad one;
"Here is frankincense," saith he,
All in cinnamon.

Saith the king in scarlet cloak,
Standing there at door;
"Here is myrrh, a bitter thing,
Kept for you of yore."

LIZETTE WOODWORTH REESE

CHRISTMAS NIGHT

My door is open wide tonight,
The hearth fire is aglow.
I seem to hear swift passing feet,
The Christ-child in the snow.

My door is open wide tonight,
For stranger, kith or kin,
I would not bar a single door
Where love might enter in.

KATE DOUGLAS WIGGIN

THE OXEN

Christmas Eve, and twelve of the clock.
"Now they are all on their knees,"
An elder said as we sat in a flock
By the embers in hearthside ease.

We pictured the meek mild creatures where
They dwelt in their strawy pen,
Nor did it occur to one of us there
To doubt they were kneeling then.

So fair a fancy few would weave
In these years! Yet, I feel,
If some one said on Christmas Eve,
"Come; see the oxen kneel

"In the lonely barton by yonder coomb
Our childhood used to know,"
I should go with him in the gloom,
Hoping it might be so.

THOMAS HARDY

THE SECRET

I go in vesture spun by hands
Upon no loom of earth,
I dwell within a shining house
That has no walls nor hearth.

I live on food more exquisite
Than honey of the bee,
More delicate than manna
It fails to nourish me.

But none may see my shining house,
Nor taste my food so rare,
And none may see my moon-spun robe
Nor my star-powdered hair.

JESSIE B. RITTENHOUSE

WHITE MAGIC

Blind folk see the fairies,
  Oh, better far than we,
Who miss the shining of their wings
Because our eyes are filled with things
  We do not wish to see.

They need not seek enchantment
  In solemn, printed books,
For all about them as they go
The fairies flutter to and fro
  With smiling, friendly looks.

Deaf folk hear the fairies
  However soft their song;
'Tis we who lose the honey sound
Amid the clamour all around
  That beats the whole day long.

But they with gentle faces
  Sit quietly apart;
What room have they for sorrowing
While fairy minstrels sit and sing
  Close to their listening heart?

Rose Fyleman

LYRIC FROM "THE LAND OF HEART'S DESIRE"

The wind blows out of the gates of day,
The wind blows over the lonely of heart,
And the lonely of heart is withered away,
While the fairies dance in a place apart,
Shaking their milk-white feet in a ring,
Shaking their milk-white arms in the air,
For they hear the wind laugh, and murmur and sing
Of a land where even the old are fair,
And even the wise are merry of tongue;
But I heard a reed of Coolaney say,
"When the wind has laughed and murmured and sung,
The lonely of heart is withered away."

William Butler Yeats

THE SONG OF WANDERING AENGUS

I went out to the hazel wood,
Because a fire was in my head,
And cut and peeled a hazel wand,
And hooked a berry to a thread;
And when white moths were on the wing,
And moth-like stars were flickering out,
I dropped the berry in a stream
And caught a little silver trout.

When I had laid it on the floor
I went to blow the fire a-flame,
But something rustled on the floor,
And some one called me by my name:
It had become a glimmering girl
With apple blossom in her hair
Who called me by my name and ran
And faded through the brightening air.

Though I am old and wandering
Through hollow lands and hilly lands,
I will find out where she has gone,
And kiss her lips and take her hands;
And walk among long dappled grass,
And pluck till time and times are done
The silver apples of the moon,
The golden apples of the sun.

WILLIAM BUTLER YEATS

PEACOCKS

Peacocks sweep the fairies' rooms;
They use their folded tails for brooms;
But fairy dust is brighter far
Than any mortal colours are;
And all about their tails it clings
In strange designs of rounds and rings;
And that is why they strut about
And proudly spread their feathers out.

ROSE FYLEMAN

THE SORCERESS!

I asked her, "Is Aladdin's lamp
Hidden anywhere?"
"Look into your heart," she said,
"Aladdin's lamp is there."

She took my heart with glowing hands.
It burned to dust and air
And smoke and rolling thistledown
Blowing everywhere.

"Follow the thistledown," she said,
"Till doomsday, if you dare,
Over the hills and far away.
Aladdin's lamp is there."

VACHEL LINDSAY

ORPHEUS WITH HIS LUTE

Orpheus with his lute made trees,
And the mountain tops that freeze,
    Bow themselves when he did sing:
To his music, plants and flowers
Ever sprung; as sun and showers
    There had made a lasting spring.

Every thing that heard him play,
Even the billows of the sea,
    Hung their heads, and then lay by.
In sweet music is such art,
Killing care and grief of heart
    Fall asleep or, hearing, die.

WILLIAM SHAKESPEARE

FAIRY BREAD

Come up here, O dusty feet,
Here is fairy bread to eat.
Here is my retiring room,
Children, you may dine
On the golden smell of broom
And the shade of pine;
And when you have eaten well,
Fairy stories hear and tell.

ROBERT LOUIS STEVENSON

FAIRY RING

I stepped within the fairy ring,
  Where it was green, so green.
Then I heard the trill of a fairy bell,
  And the song of the Fairy Queen.

The secret that she murmured me,
  To the trill of the fairy bell,
Was sweet, so sweet you'd not believe,
  If I should try to tell.

But step you too in the fairy ring,
  And hold fast to my hand;
Then we may hear a lovelier thing,
  And both will understand.

ABBIE FARWELL BROWN

THE FAIRIES HAVE NEVER A PENNY TO SPEND

The fairies have never a penny to spend,
They haven't a thing put by,
But theirs is the dower of bird and of flower
And theirs are the Earth and the Sky.
And though you should live in a palace of gold
Or sleep in a dried-up ditch,
You could never be poor as the fairies are,
And never as rich.
Since ever and ever the world began
They have danced like a ribbon of flame,
They have sung their song through the
Centuries long
And yet it is never the same.
And though you be foolish or though
You be wise,
With hair of silver or gold,
You could never be young as the fairies are,
And never as old.

ROSE FYLEMAN

I'D LOVE TO BE A FAIRY'S CHILD

Children born of fairy stock
Never need for shirt or frock,
Never want for food or fire,
Always get their heart's desire:
Jingle pockets full of gold,
Marry when they're seven years old.
Every fairy child may keep
Two strong ponies and ten sheep;
All have houses, each his own,
Built of brick or granite stone;
They live on cherries, they run wild—
I'd love to be a fairy's child.

ROBERT GRAVES

THE PIPER

Piping down the valleys wild,
    Piping songs of pleasant glee,
On a cloud I saw a child,
    And he laughing said to me:

"Pipe a song about a lamb."
    So I piped with merry cheer.
"Piper, pipe that song again";
    So I piped; he wept to hear.

"Drop thy pipe, thy happy pipe,
    Sing thy songs of happy cheer";
So I sang the same again,
    While he wept with joy to hear.

"Piper, sit thee down and write
    In a book that all may read—"
So he vanished from my sight;
    And I plucked a hollow reed,

And I made a rural pen,
    And I stain'd the water clear,
And I wrote my happy songs,
    Every child may joy to hear.

WILLIAM BLAKE

PAN

He knows the safe ways and unsafe
And he will lead the lambs to fold,
Gathering them with his merry pipe,
The gentle and the overbold.

He counts them over one by one,
And leads them back by cliff and steep,
To grassy hills where dawn is wide,
And they may run and skip and leap.

And just because he loves the lambs
He settles them for rest at noon,
And plays them on his oaten pipe
The very wonder of a tune.

FRANCIS LEDWIDGE

SEA-FEVER

I must go down to the seas again, to the lonely sea and the sky,
And all I ask is a tall ship and a star to steer her by,
And the wheel's kick and the wind's song, and the white sail's
    shaking,
And a gray mist on the sea's face and a gray dawn breaking.

I must go down to the seas again, for the call of the running tide
Is a wild call and a clear call that may not be denied;
And all I ask is a windy day with the white clouds flying,
And the flung spray and the blown spume, and the seagulls crying.

I must go down to the seas again to the vagrant gypsy life,
To the gull's way and the whale's way, where the wind's like a
    whetted knife;
And all I ask is a merry yarn from a laughing fellow rover,
And a quiet sleep and a sweet dream when the long trick's over.

JOHN MASEFIELD

IDLE AFTERNOON

I watched two little waves
Marching to the shore,
One died with a yawn,
The second with a roar,

WILLIAM SAPHIER

SHIPS IN HARBOR

I have not known a quieter thing than ships,
Nor any dreamer steeped in dreams as these;
For all that they have tracked disastrous seas,
And winds that left their sails in flagging strips;
Nothing disturbs them now, no stormy grips
That once had hurt their sides, no crash or swell;
Nor can the fretful harbor quite dispel
The quiet that they learned on lonely trips.
They have no part in all the noisy noons;
They are become as dreams of ships that go
Back to the secret waters that they know,
Each as she will, to unforgot lagoons,
Where nothing moves except her ghostly spars
That mark the patient watches on the stars.

DAVID MORTON

THE MAGIC OF THE SEA ROAD

I remember the black wharves and the ships
And the sea-tides tossing free,
And the Spanish sailors with bearded lips,
And the beauty and mystery of the ships
And the magic of the sea.

HENRY WADSWORTH LONGFELLOW

OF SEA-FOLK

Sea-Folk who once have listened to the sea
  Can never quite forget the sound of rain,
Always they hear spray falling by a tree,
  Always the sound of spray against the pane.
And so they lie out long nights listening
  For sound of water moving suddenly
And so they cannot sleep for wondering
  How many ships are anchored in a quay.
They who have once seen luggers in a bay.
  They who have once seen schooners from a hill,
  Are held by sight of many a vessel still—
Their lips are always salty for sea-spray,
  And so they cannot sleep, but lie and moan
  For things that will not leave them quite alone.

HAROLD VINAL

WINDOW SONG

There's a ship lying in and I'd like to be aboard her.
  They're loading her with iron rails and cargo for the South.
The water-line is rising with iron that they're loading,
  Down at the docks just inside the harbor mouth.

They'll be sailing in the morning with the black smoke flying
  Back with the head-wind that meets the city smoke,
Blue water rippling with the long swells behind her
  Marking out the path of the blue water folk.

There's a ship lying in and I'd like to be aboard her,
  Sailing in the morning with her hold full of rails—
Somewhere, long ago, I stood watching at a window
  Men loading cargo, and a harbor full of sails.

NANCY SHORES

Afar the ocean sleeps; white fishing-gulls
Flit where the strand is purple with its tribe
Of nested limpets; savage creatures seek
Their loves in wood and plain—and God renews
His ancient rapture!

ROBERT BROWNING

GOING DOWN IN SHIPS

Going down to sea in ships
  Is a glorious thing,
Where up and over the rolling waves
  The sea-birds wing;

Oh, there's nothing more to my heart's desire
  Then a ship that plows
Head-on down through the marching seas,
  With streaming bows.

HARRY KEMP

SEA QUATRAINS

Too fast the silly white-caps run
  Their helter-skelter races;
They stumble when the goal is won
  And fall upon their faces.

A purple light is shaken over
  The greener ocean shadows,
Like clover in the cooler depths
  Of grass in upland meadows.

The sea hangs kelp upon the sand
  Like garlands on a grave,
Mourning the dead and silent land
  With every living wave.

The breakers thunder in the night
  With white the sea is drenched.
Only one plunging line is white;
  Even the stars are quenched.

The fairest ship ever a wreck
  Had not so white a sail
As this fair wave cast up to break,
  Driven before the gale.

GRANT HYDE CODE

CARGOES

Quinquireme of Nineveh from distant Ophir,
Rowing home to haven in sunny Palestine,
  With a cargo of ivory
  And apes and peacocks,
Sandalwood, cedarwood, and sweet, white wine.

Stately Spanish galleon coming from the Isthmus,
Dipping through the Tropics by the palm-green shores
  With a cargoe of diamonds,
  Emeralds, amethysts,
Topazes, and cinnamon, and gold moidores.

Dirty British coaster with a salt-caked smoke stack
Butting through the channel in the mad March days
  With a cargo of Tyne coal,
  Road rails, pig lead,
Firewood, ironware, and cheap tin trays.

JOHN MASEFIELD

SONG FROM "THE TEMPEST"

Full fathom five thy father lies;
  Of his bones are coral made;
Those are pearls that were his eyes.
  Nothing of him that doth fade,
But doth suffer a sea-change
Into something rich and strange.
Sea nymphs hourly ring his knells—
          Ding-dong.
Hark! now I hear them,—
          Ding-dong, bell.

WILLIAM SHAKESPEARE

WINDLASS SONG

Heave at the windlass! Heave O cheerily, men!
  Heave all at once, with a will!
    The tide quickly making,
    Our courage a-creaking,
  The water has put on a frill,
    Heave O!

WILLIAM ALLINGHAM

ON FIRST SEEING THE OCEAN

And this is the dreamed-of wonder!
This—at last—is the sea!
Billows of liquid thunder—
Vocal immensity!
But where is the thrill of glory
Born of a great surprise?
This is the old, old story;
These are the ancient skies.

Child of the prairie expanses,
Often the soul of me
Hungered for long sea-glances;
And here—at last—is the sea.
Yon goes a sea-gull flying;
There is a sinking mast;
This is the ocean crying!
This is the tune of the Vast!

JOHN G. NEIHARDT

OLD SHIPS

There is a memory stays upon old ships,
A weightless cargo in the musty hold,
Of bright lagoons and prow-caressing lips,
Of stormy midnights,—and a tale untold.
They have remembered islands in the dawn,
And windy capes that tried their slender spars,
And tortuous channels where their keels have gone
And calm blue nights of stillness and the stars.

Ah, never think that ships forget a shore,
Or bitter seas, or winds, that made them wise;
There is a dream upon them, evermore;
And there be some who say that sunk ships rise
To seek familiar harbors in the night,
Blowing in mists, their spectral sails like light.

DAVID MORTON

THE SEA GYPSY

I am fevered with the sunset,
    I am fretful with the bay,
For the wander-thirst is on me
    And my soul is in Cathay.

There's a schooner in the offing,
    With her topsails shot with fire,
And my heart has gone aboard her
    For the Islands of Desire.

I must forth again tomorrow!
    With the sunset I must be
Hull-down on the trail of rapture
    In the wonder of the sea.

                    RICHARD HOVEY

THEY THAT GO DOWN TO THE SEA IN SHIPS

They that go down to the sea in ships,
And occupy their business in great waters,
These men seek the works of the Lord,
And His wonders in the deep.

For at His word the stormy wind ariseth;
Which lifteth up the waves thereof.
They are carried up to the heaven and down again to the deep;
Their soul melteth away because of the trouble.
They reel to and fro, and stagger like a drunken man;
And are at their wit's end.

When they cry unto the Lord in their trouble,
He delivereth them out of their distress.
For He maketh the storm to cease,
So that the waves thereof are still.

Then are they glad because they are at rest;
And He bringeth them unto the haven where they would be.
Oh that men would therefore praise the Lord for His goodness,
And declare the wonders that He doeth for the children of men.

                    FROM PSALM CVII

ROMANCE

I saw a ship a-sailing,
   A-sailing on the sea;
Her masts were of the shining gold,
   Her decks of ivory;
And sails of silk, as soft as milk,
   And silvern shrouds had she.

And round about her sailing,
   The sea was sparkling white,
The waves all clapped their hands and sang
   To see so fair a sight.
They kissed her twice, they kissed her thrice,
   And murmured with delight.

Then came the gallant captain,
   And stood upon the deck;
In velvet coat, and ruffles white,
   Without a spot or speck;
And diamond rings, and triple strings
   Of pearls around his neck.

And four-and-twenty sailors
   Were round him bowing low;
On every jacket three times three
   Gold buttons in a row;
And cutlasses down to their knees;
   They made a goodly show.

And then the ship went sailing,
   A-sailing o'er the sea;
She dived beyond the setting sun,
   But never back came she,
For she found the lands of the golden sands,
   Where the pearls and diamonds be.

GABRIEL SETOUN

Whirl up, sea—
Whirl your pointed pines.
Splash your great pines
On your rocks.
Hurl your green over us—
Cover us with your pools of fir.

H. D.

FROM APOSTROPHE TO THE OCEAN

Roll on, thou deep and dark blue Ocean—roll!
Ten thousand fleets sweep over thee in vain;
Man marks the earth with ruin—his control
Stops with the shore;—upon the watery plain.
The wrecks are all thy deed, nor doth remain
A shadow of man's ravage, save his own,
When, for a moment, like a drop of rain,
He sinks into thy depth with bubbling groan,
Without a grave, unknelled, uncoffined, and unknown.

His steps are not upon thy paths,—thy fields
Are not spoil for him,—thou dost arise
And shake him from thee; the vile strength he wields
For earth's destruction thou dost all despise,
Spurning him from thy bosom to the skies,
And send'st him, shivering in thy playful spray,
And howling, to his Gods, where haply lies
His petty hope in some near port or bay,
And dashest him again to earth:—there let him lay.

Thou glorious mirror, where the Almighty's form
Glasses itself in tempests; in all time,
Calm or convulsed—in breeze, or gale, or storm,
Icing the pole, or in the torrid clime
Dark-heaving;—boundless, endless, and sublime—
The image of Eternity—the throne
Of the Invisible; even from out thy slime
The monsters of the deep are made; each zone
Obeys thee; thou goest forth, dread, fathomless, alone.

And I have loved thee, Ocean! and my joy
Of youthful sports was on thy breast to be
Borne, like thy bubbles, onward: from a boy
I wantoned with thy breakers—they to me
Were a delight; and if the freshening sea
Made them a terror—'twas a pleasing fear,
For I was, as it were, a child of thee,
And trusted to thy billows far and near,
And laid my hand upon thy mane—as I do here.

From "Childe Harold's Pilgrimage" by
LORD BYRON

POEMS FROM THE SANDALWOOD BOX

*T*he campers and counselors who have helped compile this collection of poetry often put their own thoughts into verse. In the wide eaves of one of their favorite cabins is a Sandalwood Box in which they place their poems. On Sunday the little box is taken to evening fire and the contents read to the group. We include in the following pages a few of the poems and songs which have come from the Sandalwood Box. In these are expressed the interests, enthusiasm and ideals of the Four Winds and Westward Ho campers.

Because life shines and sings to me
I need not ride great ships to sea;
I need not even take a train,
To distant lands of storied fame.

All I need do is fling my door
Open to the wind and shore,
Open to the sky and sea,
And all the world comes in to me!

R. A. B.

THE QUEST

Today I searched for God, mother.
You said, "He is everywhere."
I looked, mother, through the garden
And upon a high hill
I listened,
But at sunset He had not come,
Though the gate was wide.
So I brought these pussywillows to you,
And the river is high
With new grass on its banks;
A thrush sang, mother,
But I could not find God.

R. A. B.

NIGHT

Translucent wisps of cloud lift across the moon—
Big, round, white coin wrapped in silver lace.

H. E. G.

THE VEGETABLE COUNTER

Orange carrots with fringed green hair,
Bunched among yellow striped beans,
Bright red beets and yellow squash
Crisp wet lettuce and spinach greens.

Purple eggplant with silver onions,
Red cheeked apples catch the eye,
Furry peaches and scarlet peppers,
Odd shaped gourds hung up to dry.

                                    J. A. N.

THOUGHT

Tiny perfect flower,
    Every petal true,
I can see a whole world
    Complete in you.

Rising, budding, blooming
    Giving seed, and then
Wilting and returning
    To the earth again.

                                    L. C. F.

SNOW

God's up in heaven shearing his sheep.
He's making a blanket four inches deep
To cover the earth with,
To keep out the cold;
One by one he's shearing his fold.
He's scattering the wool bits all over the land;
Softly, silently, they fall from his hand.

                                    H. H.

RAIN

That wretch, the Rain,
Is a saucy wench;
She mocks me with
Her silver eyes.

She blears my pane
With kisses white
And clutches at
My fireside ties.

Fat books are vain
And strives to wrest
My thoughts away
From Rain's sweet lies.

On logic sane
She casts a glance
With scorn full-fraught,
Ah, Rain defies

My acts mundane.
But when I flee
From warm content,
Her glamor dies.

HELEN GRAY

THE NEW MOON

The afternoon had a secret that
    almost nobody knew;
A tall pine pointed it out to me,
    a finger raised toward the blue.
Hid in a soft white cloudlet over
    the still dark pine
Lay the fairies' silvery sailboat—
    the new moon
Waiting to shine.

MARTHA LADD

GARGOYLES

Gargoyles
On a building
Look down
Through the rush of day,
Through the hush of night,
They grin
At little people.
Sometimes, when no one looks,
The cold rain
Falls from their eyes
In murky tears.

G. M.

WORDS

Many things I love
But of all things beautiful
Words—
Words that go buttoned
In little gray cloaks;
You undo the cloaks,
And swish!
Shining beauty
Comes out.

R. A. B.

TIDES

Tides—pushing, pulling—
A silver ribbon in the blue sound.

NANCY BISSEL

HER VOICE

Her voice was like a crystal stream
Sparkling in the sun;
Here a ripple, there a ripple,
Here a little run.

It laughed along the hill of life,
Through the forest deep and dark;
Here a gurgle, there a gurgle,
Here a splashing lark.

And many a weary traveller
Has heard its gay refrain
And gone away refreshed with music
Singing in his brain.

The sweetest tunes, the gayest tunes,
So happy and so true;
Here a bubble, there a bubble,
Here a bubble, too.

Until one day a sorrow came,
A jagged rock it made,
And broke the gladness of her voice
Into a white cascade.
It plunged the singing waters to
The bottom of the hill,
And there they formed a deep, deep pool,
All shadowy and still.

It does not bubble anymore,
But neither does it sigh.
It lies a limpid mirror for
The beauty of the sky.

MARTHA LADD

Each butterfly the secret knows,
Each blade of grass, and tree;
And only man is unaware
Of his identity.

FANNY MARGARET MORRILL

LIFE

Life, fill my hands I cried
And held them wide,
And casually from an ample store
Life filled them o'er.

R. A. B.

A SEAGULL'S FLIGHT

Seagull's wings have swept the sky today,
  Their sleek greyed feathers cut the clouds and pass
With that half whispered chant of fear and glee
  The listening have heard in wind-tossed grass.

Oh, for the freedom of the seagull's flight!
  Touching dawn and evening with soft wings,
Seeking waves be-calmed to glassy peace,
  Knowing storms with cold, and salt spray stings.

Leaded hearts hold mortals to the earth—
Only seagulls know a sunset's worth.

G. S.

AUTUMN

Under my feet the gay leaves crackle,
And shadows make patterns along the way,
While high over head the geese are passing,
Though it's warm and sweet as a summer's day.

It's warm and sweet, but well I'm knowing
That summer is over and autumn come;
I can tell it by the gold leaves blowing
And the slow, warm touch of the August sun.

R. A. B.

GYPSY BREAD

The gypsy's hearth is a wide, wide hearth
And its warmth he'll always share.
The bread he bakes is friendly bread
And he gives it to all who fare.
For those who follow the wide world o'er
Have need of friendly bread,
Bread of daring and laughter and courage high
And nothing can take its stead.
Who will follow the highroad and
Trailways with me o'er the world
In quest of the gypsy bread!

R. A. B.

LAUGHTER

Laughter runs by in silver sandals shining,
Stops in at every wide-flung, friendly door.
Warm be the gypsy fires that we keep burning,
That laughter may stay ever more.

R. A. B.

STAR SONG

Up the tallest hill together
We shall climb until on high;
We can watch the constellations
March across the summer sky.

Deep down in the bay below us
Lie great pools of starry gold;
May our hearts one day unknowing
Such reflected beauty hold.

R. A. B.

MORNING SONG

Far down the mountain the new day has come,
Gray scarves of dawning slip out to sea;
Loveliness waits on the threshold again—
Softly she calls to me.

Let us arise and go running to meet her,
Catch at the stars that she shakes from her hair;
Bathe in the gold she has spilled in the meadow,
For gypsies must follow where e'er she may fare.

Shimmering ribbons of color are thrown
Far over meadow and mountain and sea,
Loveliness laughs from the top of the world,
Softly she calls to me.

                                    R. A. B.

THE HEATHER IS BLOWING

The heather is blowing and bending in the sun,
The marmots will tell you a new day has begun,
So up with the sunrise and let's be on the way—
Take laughter with you on the trail today.

We'll climb up the mountains with wings on our feet,
Crispy winds will blow us toward distant Cascade peaks.
The brooklets will sing you a merry mountain air,
Oh, happiness walks hand in hand with a mountaineer.

                          ELIZABETH PRITCHARD JACOBSEN

THE CHORUS TO "VICTORIA SONG"

Victoria is waiting
Just across the sea,
With shops all full of old antiques
And the Empress full of tea.
If you long for England's shore
You'll find it very near.
Victoria is famous
For its British atmosphere.

                          ELIZABETH PRITCHARD JACOBSEN

WHOEVER HAS KNOWN THE MOUNTAINS

Whoever has known the mountains,
The forest, the sky and the sea,
Warmth of the friendly camp fire,
Strength of the winds that blow free;
The color and fragrance of meadows,
The lilt of a sudden song,
His are the gifts worth having,
Treasures to last a life long,
These are the treasures worth having
Shining, enduring and strong.

Whoever has climbed to the hilltops
And called all the stars by name,
Who loves balsam odors of summer
And the silver singing of rain;
Oh, life will be always adventure
Though his trails may take him afar,
And warmth and friendship and laughter
He'll find 'neath the gypsy star,
Oh, all the gifts of the wide world
Wait under the gypsy star.

R. A. B.—H. W. B.

THE GYPSY STAR

Well do I love the trail,
Well do I love the sea,
Stars and the hills at night
Reach out and clutch at me.

Though I may stay at home,
My doors are open wide,
The world comes in to me
Full like the morning tide.

Some there are who wander
Over seas and lands afar,
But through my window
Shines the Gypsy Star.

R. A. B.

OH, WINDS THAT BLOW

Oh, winds that blow across the sea and mountains,
Oh, flying winds that stir the heart of me,
A boon today I would of you be asking,
A boon to set this gypsy spirit free;
For I should like to follow where you call me,
And I would gladly lace my gypsy sandals very tight,
And all the winds and storms I would be daring,
Or push my laughing way across the starry night.

But after I have gone so far a-wandering,
I'll very quickly turn my sandals home,
And from my way the stars I shall be brushing,
It must be always so with those who roam.
But starry wonder still will stay beside me,
And gypsy winds will blow the leaves about my
        friendly door,
Yet well I know that one day I'll be going
To chase a silver star across a lonely moor.

                                    R. A. B.

VAGABOND'S SONG

Far I long to go today,
Where my heart is ever turning,
Far, to where the seagulls cry,
To the hills with sunset burning.

There bright shines the starry sky,
Soft the winds with salt spray blowing,
There along the friendly shore,
Full and free the tide is flowing.

Fair the lands that 'round me lie,
But fairer land I'm knowing;
Hills and sea are calling me,
And one day I shall be going.

                                    R. A. B.

THE SEAGULL

I saw a seagull flying
White wings against the sky,
I saw a seagull flying,
Crying its plaintive cry.

If I were that seagull flying,
Soaring against the sky,
Mine would be a joyous song,
Not a plaintive cry.

H. W. B.

TWILIGHT FALLS

Twilight falls,
Dusky shadows steal
Over murmuring waters,
Down the quiet hillsides.
Four Winds' peace
Dwells in every heart,
As the evening breezes
Lull us to rest.

ALICE BALDWIN

NIGHT SONG

Off to rest, off to rest,
And may sweet be thy dreaming,
Down the trailways of the night,
Up the moon's great path of light;
Lit with laughter and peace
Oh, may fair be thy journeying!
Till the songs of the day
Send night softly away.

R. A. B.

THE SNARE

I hear a sudden cry of pain!
There is a rabbit in a snare,
Now I hear the cry again,
But I cannot tell from where . . .

But I cannot tell from where
He is calling out for aid!
Crying on the frightened air,
Making everything afraid . . .

Making everything afraid,
Wrinkling up his little face
As he cries again for aid,
And I cannot find the place . . .

And I cannot find the place
Where his paw is in the snare.
Little one! Oh, little one!
I am searching everywhere . . .

PETER WOOLSTON

AROUND THE CAMPFIRE

Little campers round their blaze,
    Always listen in a daze,
To grownups whose strange tales unfold,
    Of phantoms lurking and knights so bold.
Of funny things and solemn too,
    Of knights that often dragons slew,
Of all those things in those old days,
    They listen to around their blaze.

RALPH ROGERS

True friends are like diamonds
Precious and rare,
False ones are like autumn leaves
Found everywhere.

SALLY SMITH

POWER

The Sea roars on.
   People love and people hate.
The Sea roars on.
   Rocks turn to sand and
Boys turn to men.

The Sea roars on.
   People live and people die.
The Sea roars on.
   A friendship lasts and
The Sea does too.

The Sea roars on.
   All others change
But never these two.
   The Sea roars on.

DAN MARSHALL

THE GRASS IS LIKE A FREEWAY

The grass is like a Freeway
All trampled down.
The bugs and flies go crawling
In and out of the ground.
The trees are made of weeds,
The bridges made of grass.
All the little insects wave as they pass.

The grass is like a Freeway
And every car that passes
Sees highways made of grasses.
The cars are made of bugs
Yellow, green and red.
The worms are like trolley cars
With double deckers instead.

The grass is like a Freeway
With buzzing all about
As each little bug car
Goes streaming in and out.

MARY JANE HELSELL AND CAROLE BRECK

BEFORE THE RAIN

The air is warm and very still
Across the bay the crow's cry, shrill.
One crisp, dry leaf drops slowly down
To join its mates that strew the ground.
Clouds gathered over isle and sea
Bring warning of a storm to be.
The gray-blue smoke of camp fire near
Drifts toward the sky—and soft! we hear
The silver, sound of rain!

ANONYMOUS

THE COMING RAIN

There was expectancy in the air,
As if the whole world was holding its breath.
Waiting for something;
It knew not what.
Waiting . . . . Waiting . . . .

And then it came.
First one timid drop, and then another
Until it was a torrent.
The earth let out its breath,
And the waiting was over.

J. M.

RAIN

Silver grey the cool rain falls.
Parched Earth, who has dragged through
An eternity of days
Drinks thirstily.
The dry roadside flowers lift tired faces,
And are washed.
Deep in the forest, where no wind has come
For many days,
The pines, clean smelling, lift and stir once more.
The rain is here.

ANONYMOUS

SECRET PLACE

I know a quiet place
  Where I like to be,
Whenever I want to think
  Or when I am feeling Lonely.
This place is a big rock,
  Looking over the sea,
And when I am there
  I feel strength in me.
I dangle my feet
  Over the side,
And feel the water
  Splash up from the tide.
Fish swim by
  And look up at me,
And I smile back
  At them in the sea.
I can feel the sun
  Shining down on my back,
Making my shadow
  A shade of black.
I took a guitar
  And played it there once,
But I rather prefer
  The still silence . . . .

At my quiet place.

KIM LAR RIEU

DONUTS

It's fun to make donuts
In a great big pot.
When we ring the bell,
An awful lot,
Of campers come running
Up the hill,
To find the donuts
And eat their fill.

ANONYMOUS

REMEMBRANCES

Some things impress upon the human
    mind
A picture, sometimes vivid, sometimes
    dull.
Scarlet poppies along a rambling path,
Stately yellow hollyhocks along a
    prim garden walk,
Mountains seen at sunset through a
    veil of sun gold,
A frail, spider's web silhouetted
    against a full moon,
The Northern Lights flaring up into
    the midnight sky.
Silver phosphorous gleaming faintly
    in black waters,
Grey ocean moving restlessly, over-
    shadowed by ominous clouds,
Cool, damp earth between bare toes,
The pungent odor of hay at evening,
Glowing embers like a magic fairy's
    castle—
These and many more will live forever
    in my memory's gallery.

LEATRICE GILBERT

These acres I have known for years,
Yet every day to me more dear
They grow, and I could not say why
I love that stone, or piece of sky
I see when I sit in this place,
And so familiar is the face
Of that blue hill across the sound,
So well I know, if I turn 'round,
That twisting, red madrona tree
And rocky island I will see!
Each curve of wind, each spot of sun,
Each grassy slope where breezes run,
The changes that new seasons bring,
The tantalizing smell of spring,
The winter's wind and autumn's gold—
All these within my heart I hold.

F. M. M.

REMEMBERING

I shall remember dogwood in the spring,
All starry-eyed;
And sunlight sifting through the trees
Off trailways wide.
I shall remember always myriad things
That I once knew,
Gnarled old apple trees, Queen Anne's Lace,
And waters blue.

Blue smoke at twilight I shall follow up a hill,
All evening till
With night's blue peace of earth and sea and sky
My heart will fill;
And when the new moon drenches all the trees
In new delight,
Back I shall turn to golden candlelight
And kindly night.

R. A. B.

LOVELINESS REMEMBERED

This loveliness shall never die:
Above the hill of fir points high
Full moon a-sail through rain-washed sky,

And in the orchard grass below,
Small, crooked paths where children go
A treasure seeking, to and fro;

Red coals, where cabin fires have been,
A bird song, far, flute-fine and thin,
The sound of night tide coming in;

Slow rain that splatters off the eaves,
Wet fox glove, sheltering honey thieves,
Moist trails all strewn with yellow leaves;

An evening hearth fire, high and bright,
The sound of singing in the night,
A friend's face in the candle light.

These things can never die for me;
As long as lives my memory
Such loveliness shall ever be.

MARY JEFFRIES

GIFTS

The nicest things in life are those
Which money cannot buy—
For what price has a silver star
Or flaming sunset sky?

At what market place or stall
Can one buy autumn hills,
Or pools of rock which each new tide
With crystal coolness fills?

A. B.

I must not hurry along this road
There is too much to see:
A crimson flower, a wrinkled toad,
A knotty scarred oak tree;
A bubbling brook, a lacy fern,
A cobweb shimmering still,
A yellow bird whose mournful notes,
Sound over the vale and hill.

Because all nature's loveliness
Is very dear to me,
I must not hurry along this road
There is too much to see.

JULIE HOVER

SIMPLE TREASURES

Queens and kings
search for things
like gold and jewels and crowns.
But all alone
in a peasant's home
a different treasure is found.
A treasure of joy and peace
and love that never fails—
For what good is the greatest treasure
if evil and greed prevail?

SARAH SHERWOOD

WALKING IN THE WOODS

I like to walk alone sometimes
    among the tallest trees,
And listen to the birds and
    feel the cool and gentle breeze;
I like to sit upon green moss
    and think of quiet things,
Awaiting all the happiness
    that summer always brings;
And when I leave, my mind
    is full of beauty quite serene,
Remembering all the wonders
    that my eager eyes have seen.

KRIS METCALFE

I am the tallest pine on the hill.
Below,
Shape of island
Curve of beach
And the sea.

Above,
Shape of clouds
Sound of gull
And the wind.

The wind moves through
Making sound of me
And I am soothed.

DOROTHY WEBSTER LUNDBLAD

INDEX OF FIRST LINES

AUTHOR INDEX

YOUR OWN SPECIAL POEMS AND SONGS

OUR OWN SPECIAL POEMS AND SONGS

YOUR OWN SPECIAL POEMS AND SONGS